HAWAIIAN APPLIQUÉ

Vicky Fleming

D1558395

American Quilter's Society
P. O. Box 3290 • Paducah, KY 42002-3290
www.AQSquilt.com

Located in Paducah, Kentucky, the American Quilter's Society (AQS) is dedicated to promoting the accomplishments of today's quilters. Through its publications and events, AQS strives to honor today's quiltmakers and their work and to inspire future creativity and innovation in quiltmaking.

EDITOR: TRACEY JOHNSON
GRAPHIC DESIGN: AMY CHASE
COVER DESIGN: MICHAEL BUCKINGHAM
PHOTOGRAPHY: CHARLES R. LYNCH

Library of Congress Cataloging-in-Publication Data

Fleming, Vicky.
    Hawaiian applique / by Vicky Fleming.
        p. cm.
        ISBN 1-57432-837-9
    1. Appliqué--Patterns. 2. Quilting--Patterns. 3. Quilts--Hawaii.
I. Title.

TT779.F73 2004
746.46'041--dc22
                        2003026161

Additional copies of this book may be ordered from the American Quilter's Society, PO Box 3290, Paducah, KY 42002-3290, or online at www.AQSquilt.com.

Aloha! Aloha.

This is perhaps my favorite word in any language. Besides the "hello" and "goodbye" meanings taught at the tourist luaus, *aloha* traditionally and truly means "love." It means "good wishes to you" and "God be with you." It is a kind message, a loving wish for well being, a friendly greeting. So, *aloha* to you. Join me in quilting traditionally styled Hawaiian wall quilts. I will share with you sixteen patterns for my original designs, plus ten original pillow-sized patterns. I will show you how to make these quilts in the traditional manner and share with you the *kaona*, or secret meaning, behind some of the designs.

What I ask of you in return is that you take the time to stitch these pieces by hand. This is important. There is "good medicine" in making a Hawaiian quilt in the traditional way. It is good for your mind and your spirit to sit quietly and do repetitive motions while creating something beautiful. If you also give some thought to the gentler lifestyle of Hawaii, perhaps you will find ways to incorporate that into your own life, making your own world a more serene place. In the end, you will find that the making of the quilt was more meaningful than having the completed project, beautiful as it is. Furthermore, as you stitch you will be putting your own *mana*, or spirit, into your quilt. The whole point of making a Hawaiian quilt is to express your *aloha* in a tactile way. I believe that if you will give yourself to the making of a Hawaiian quilt in the traditional way, you will be pleased with the results, both in your hands and in your heart.

Acknowledgments

Mahalo nui loa (a great big thank you) to these people, who in one way or another made this book possible:

To my mother, who taught me how to sew at a very early age (I was making tailored garments by age twelve).

To my father, who told me I could do anything I wanted to if I was willing to work for it.

To my husband, who provided the "space" for me to become a full-time quilter and now an author.

To Marge Kerr, my first *kupuna* (Hawaiian quilting instructor). Marge faithfully passed on all she had learned from Deborah Kakalia of the Bishop Museum in Honolulu. Marge also started The Ha'ole Connection, a group of about twelve quilters from the Colorado Front Range who met once a month to quilt Hawaiian, "talk story," and share island-style foods.

To The Ha'ole Connection, which means more to me now than ever. When I think of how pivotal this group's company and encouragement were to my development as a Hawaiian quilter and as a happy person, I am forever grateful.

To Deborah Kakalia, Elizabeth Akana, Althea "Poakalani" Serrao, and so many other Hawaiian quilters who were willing to share their knowledge with outsiders.

To the Hawaiian people, without whose *aloha* the islands would be just another pretty place. It's the people, the *aloha*, that make Hawaii special.

To Pam Pampe, AQS appraiser and past president of the American Quilt Study Group, for her advice and encouragement.

To Becky Baird, who gently nudged me back on track.

And to you, for being interested in the beautiful art of Hawaiian quilting. *Mahalo*.

Preface

I truly enjoy making Hawaiian-style quilts and want to encourage and enable you to make them, too. Traditional Hawaiian quilts are stitched by hand, through many hours of relaxation and time to think. They can be bold and graceful, with bright colors and the gentle curves of *kuiki lau* (echo quilting), or they can be subtle, with softer shades and an overall quilting pattern.

I also want to record and demonstrate some of the older styles of appliqué and quilting rarely seen today. These quilting patterns can be traced back to the carved wooden mallet and stamps used to create *tapa*, a cloth made of pounded tree bark. Using these patterns gave me a sense of connection with the quilters and *tapa* artisans of old Hawai'i.

I cherish the traditional Hawaiian values, such as *aloha*, and hope this is reflected in my designs. To express *aloha* is to be kind, generous, and respectful. *Aloha* translates as "in the presence of the breath of life," which, to me, means the Hawaiians had a close relationship with the holy energy of the universe. Another translation might be "in touch with God." Hawaiians understand the interconnectedness of nature and are respectful of the land, the sea, and the plants and animals around them. They also treasure *'ohana*, the warmth of family.

Twenty years ago, when I started making Hawaiian-style quilts, there was little information outside the islands on how to do the work and which elements should or should not be included in the quilts. Few people were offering commercial patterns, and wall quilts were almost non-existent. One can only make so many Hawaiian pillows, so I began designing my own wall quilts. The patterns given here are all my original designs. A few of these were sold as pattern kits several years ago, so you may find someone who already has one of them, but many of these designs have never been published anywhere before.

It is my sincere hope that, through this book, you will be inspired and encouraged to make Hawaiian-style quilts in the traditional ways. In our fast-paced modern world, I find great comfort in taking the time to learn about Hawaiian traditions and to make Hawaiian-style quilts "the old-fashioned way."

Contents

Contents

Introduction

What is "traditional" Hawaiian quilting? These days, one thinks of the stereotypical snowflake pattern quilt, with eight segments, in two solid colors, and quilted with echo quilting. These quilts are beautiful, with their strong graphics and graceful quilting lines, but there are two more categories of Hawaiian quilts to consider: historical and contemporary.

Many of the historical quilts have very different quilting styles, such as parallel lines or grids. Some consist of five disconnected design segments (one in each of the four corners and one in the center). Some have conspicuous, fancy appliqué stitches. Hawaiian flag quilts fall into the historical category. The contemporary Hawaiian quilt category includes traditional patterns done in bold tropical prints or batiks, or any other style that honors some facet of Hawaiian life.

In this book, you will find information on the historical quilting patterns and appliqué stitches. A list of Hawaiian words and phrases is given for your information and out of respect for the Hawaiian language and culture. The bibliography lists fascinating books full of information about the history of Hawaiian quilting. If you need a little Hawaiian music to get you in the mood, I have listed some resources for music, books, video tapes, and other Hawaiian quilt patterns.

Use this book to make your own quilt by mixing and matching elements in the examples shown here. For example, you may want to do Pā 'Ana A Ka Lā in a deep purple on white with *kuiki lau* (echo quilting). I think Nā Pua Ulu Pono Me Aloha would look stunning in bright red on white. Consider your fabric and color choices, the appliqué stitch, the quilting pattern, and even the type and density of batting. These choices will add up to a quilt that is uniquely your own. You'll be quilting your *mana* (spirit energy) into the quilt, so you want it to represent your own personality.

I hope you will also use this book as a launching pad for your own research into Hawaiian quilt history and Hawaiian philosophy. That will teach you much more than I can show you here. You'll learn about more Hawaiian plants and flowers, Hawaiian history and traditions, color combinations, graphic elements, design scale, and more.

When your projects are completed and you enter them in shows or send photos to magazines, please be considerate of my copyright and give me credit for the design. I am sharing twenty years of quilting with you in the spirit of *aloha. Mahalo nui loa.*

Chapter One:
From Tapa Cloth
to Appliqué Quilts

The History of Hawaiian Quilting

When Polynesians first peopled the Hawaiian Islands, they made "cloth" by pounding the inner bark of the *wauke*, or paper mulberry tree. This cloth was called *tapa*. The *tapa* beater was a mallet, called an *I'e kuku*, which had different watermark designs carved into it. The *tapa* was decorated with drawings and stampings, and sometimes dyed with natural plant dyes. The design stamps were carved of bamboo and were called *'ohe kāpala*. The Hawaiians used bedcovers made of four plain *tapa* and a top layer, called the *kilohana*, which was dyed or stamped with a design. These five layers were stitched together at one end, and were called *kapa moe*.

After discovery of the islands by Captain James Cook in 1778, traders and whalers from around the world began stopping in Hawaii for provisions. Hawaiians were exposed to many new skills, such as fine tailoring, and acquired many new materials, such as cotton cloth and metal needles. Traders returning to America from China brought with them fine silks and chintzes. German mariners may have taught the Hawaiians the paper-cutting technique called *scherenschnitte*, which produced complex snowflake-like designs. Exposure to these western skills and materials likely impacted the techniques and styles Hawaiians used in their *kapa moe*.

When the sailing brig *Thaddeus* arrived in 1820, American missionary wife Lucy Thurston recorded in her diary that a quilting bee took place aboard ship with four high-ranking Hawaiian women. She believed it was the first quilting bee ever to take place in Hawaii. While it may have been the first time Hawaiians were taught American *patchwork*, Mrs. Thurston would have no way of knowing if the Hawaiians were skilled in making cotton versions of their *kapa moe*. She did record that among the four Hawaiian women was dowager queen Kalakua, who brought with her a quanity of white cambric (a thin cotton or linen fabric) to have a dress made in the latest western fashion. There are many popular stories of how Hawaiian quilting as we know it today got started. Some say it was with Lucy Thurston, others think a Hawaiian woman saw the shadow of a tree on a freshly laundered sheet and was inspired to trace the shadow for her design. It is my belief that today's Hawaiian quilt is part of a gradual evolution from *tapa* designs to cotton appliqué quilts.

Because the climate in Hawaii, with strong sunshine and salt air, is hard on textiles, relatively few old Hawaiian quilts remain. Also, because Hawaiians believed that one's *mana*, or spiritual power, is stitched into the quilts, some felt that their possessions, including their quilts, had to be destroyed at their death, so that their spirit would be complete. In 1990, the Hawaiian Quilt Research Project started collecting data on the remaining quilts made in Hawaii before 1959, the year Hawaii became a state.

Quilting Styles

Early quilt motifs generally were more slender than those of today's designs. The elements were often plants or flowers, but could also be objects that related to a particular event. For example, NAWILIWILI BEAUTY, by Mrs. George Montgomery of Kaua'i, has an anchor design, commemorating the opening of Nawiliwili Harbor. Several designs include items relating to the Hawaiian *ali'i*, or royalty. One particularly beautiful example is KA PIKA PUA O HALE ALI'I, a popular design ca. 1930, taken from the etched glass in the doors of 'Iolani Palace.

Many early quilts (*kapa*) were quilted with patterns other than echo quilting (*kuiki lau*). Designs such as the crisscross grid pattern (*kuiki maka 'upena*) could have come from missionary quilt examples or from the designs carved into the *tapa* tools, the *'ohe kāpala* or *i'e kuku*. Many of the surviving early quilts did not follow what we today consider the rules of how to make Hawaiian quilts. They were often made of pastel colors, sometimes with small calico prints, and appliquéd with conspicuous stitches, such as cross-stitch (*humu kā*) and chicken feet (*wāwae moa*) patterns.

Temporary English rule in 1843 led to the creation of the earliest Hawaiian flag quilts (*kapa hae*), in honor of the monarchy and as a subtle form of protest. These quilts usually took the form of four Hawaiian flags surrounding a center square. The center square usually had a variation of the official coat of arms and the words *"Ku'u hae aloha"* (My beloved flag). Sometimes the state motto, *"Ua mau ke ea o ka āina i ka pono"* ("The life of the land is perpetuated in righteousness"), declared by King David Kalakaua in 1843, is seen.

Between 1880 and 1925, embroidered quilts were popular in both Hawaii and the mainland. These were similar to what we call "redwork" in the embroidery style. They were usually quilted in some sort of grid pattern. One example by Eme Mahikoa, in the Mission Houses Museum collection, demonstrates the turtle's back (*kuiki kuahonu* or *honu ipu*) quilting pattern, which is said to have originated on Kauai.

The 1970s brought renewed interest in Hawaiian quilts, with the vast majority being stitched strictly with solid colors, hidden appliqué stitches, and echo quilting, and within restrictions (*kapu*) laid down years earlier. All of the work had to be done by hand. Patterns were designed in eighths and cut out by folding the fabric into eighths.

Contemporary Hawaiian quilting blossomed in the late 1990s. While some of these quilts are traditional patterns, but stitched in wild prints or batiks, others bear no resemblance to the old styles. They are Hawaiian quilts, however, by virtue of the fact that they honor some facet of Hawaiian life. Examples include designs of rice bowls, landscape designs of Hawaiian landmarks, or images of the whales or dolphins which live in Hawaiian waters.

The Rules

Elements of the Hawaiian belief system carry over into the realm of quilting. *Kapu* are the restrictions, things that are taboo. Certain colors or patterns are used or avoided. Rituals follow the completion of a quilt. Many quilt designs have a secret meaning, or *kaona*. I try to abide by the *kapu* when making traditional-style Hawaiian quilts. This contributes to my sense of connection with the Hawaiian quilters, past and present, who see value in the old Hawaiian ways.

Here are some of the *kapu*:

- Never use black. It is an unlucky color.

- People or animals should not be depicted. It was thought that their spirits would move about at night.

- Don't show your quilt until it is finished.

- Don't steal someone else's design.

- Don't sit on your quilt. Your *mana* is in there!

- When your quilt is completed, sleep under it one time before giving it away. This is to restore sufficient *mana* to you so that you can go on to make more *kapa*. With a wall quilt, perhaps a hug of the quilt will do.

- My personal *kapu*: When your *kapa* is finished (*pau*), silently give thanks for having the time and talent to make such a beautiful piece and thank the quilt for giving you so much pleasure.

State Motto
Ua mau ke ea o ka āina i ka pono:
The life of the land is perpetuated in righteousness.

Hawaiian Words and Phrases

Hawaiian words sometimes have markings called the *kahakō* and the *'okina*. The *kahakō* looks like a "long vowel" mark, a straight line over a vowel. We've used an accent mark here to depict the *kahakō*. This lengthens the sound of the vowel slightly. The *'okina* looks like a closed 6, but here we are using the "foot measurement" mark, ', to show the *'okina*. It is used where there is a glottal stop, as in the phrase "Oh-oh." Using these markings correctly is important. We can demonstrate with the word *aina*. *'Aina* with the *'okina* means meal; *Āina* with a *kahakō* over the first A means land.

Hawaiian vowels are pronounced: a = ah, e = long a, i = long e, o = oh, u = u as in tuna. Example: In Hawaiian, *Likelike* Highway is pronounced "Lee-kay-lee-kay" Highway.

Hala kahiki	pineapple
Honu	turtle
Honu ipu	turtle's back quilting pattern (see *Kuiki kuahonu*)
Humu	to sew, as to stitch a seam
Humu ho'oholoholo	running stitch, to baste
Humu kā	cross-stitch
Humu kaulahao	chain stitch
Humulau	to embroider
Humuwili	overcast stitch, to appliqué or hem
I'e kuku	*tapa* beater
Kahua	the quilt background
Kaona	secret meaning
Kapa	Hawaiian quilt
Kapa lau	1. one-piece design 2. appliquéd Hawaiian quilt
Kapa āpana	1. two-piece design, consisting of a center design, or *piko*, and a border design, called a *lei* 2. appliquéd Hawaiian quilt
Kapa pili	a quilt without batting

Kapa pulu	a quilt with batting
Kapa pohopoho	1. several smaller designs put together, like a sampler quilt 2. patchwork or crazy quilt
Kapu	forbidden
Kilohana	top layer of a *tapa* bed covering
Koana	the spacing between rows of quilting
Kuiki	to quilt
Kuiki hā 'ao	a zigzag quilting pattern taken from *tapa* beaters
Kuiki kuahonu	quilting in a turtle's back design (also called *honu ipu*)
Kuiki lala	diagonal quilting
Kuiki lau	echo quilting
Kuiki maka moena	quilting which resembles the weaving of a *lau hala* mat
Kuiki maka 'upena	crisscrossing lines, as in a mesh pattern (diagonal grid)
Kuiki pāpa 'a pelena	square in a square quilting design, also called whole cracker or soda cracker
Kuiki 'upena-pupu	quilting pattern of a circle within a square, in a grid pattern (also called Five Cent pattern)
Lau	the quilt design or motif
Lau hala	1. *pandanus* leaf 2. mat woven of *pandanus* leaves
Lei	1. flower or shell necklace or garland 2. border design 3. circular design
Makana	gift, donation
Makani	wind
Mana	one's spiritual power
Mana'o	thought, idea, belief, meaning

Moani	fragrant breeze
Nani	beautiful
'Ohe kāpala	bamboo stamps for marking *tapa*
Pau	finished
Piko	center
Pili	the quilt backing
Pua	flower, offspring
Pulu	batting
Tapa	inner bark of the *wauke,* or paper mulberry tree, which was beaten to make cloth
U'i	beauty
Ulu	to grow
'Ulu	breadfruit
Wāwae moa	chicken feet appliqué stitch

Island Colors and Symbols

- Hawai'i—red, *lehua,* flower of the ohi'a tree
- Kaho'olawe—gray, *hinahina,* silversword plant
- Kaua'i—purple, *mokihana,* a tree with anise-scented fruit
- Lāna'i—yellow, *kaunaoa,* a vine with orange stems
- Maui—pink, *lokelani,* rose
- Moloka'i—green, *kukui,* candlenut plant
- Ni'ihau—white, *pūpū,* shell
- O'ahu—yellow, *ilima,* a flowering shrub

Chapter Two:
General Instructions

Hawaiian-style quilting is relatively easy to do and well within your capabilities if you proceed with patience. Follow the easy steps below from start to finish in making your quilt. Take time to enjoy the feel of the fabric, to turn the appliqué smoothly, and to make your quilting evenly spaced.

Planning Your Quilt

Choose a pattern

Considerations when you are choosing a pattern include your appliqué skill level, the meaning of the design, the intended use of the piece, and your color choices. For example, you may choose to make 'Ulu, the breadfruit pattern, first. The similar word *ulu* (without the *'okina*) means "plenty," and the two meanings have been mingled in quilting, so that to do an 'Ulu first means you will go on to do more quilts. Breadfruit was a starchy staple of the early Hawaiian diet. Breadfruit is green, so appliquéing a green 'ulu design onto a white or light sky blue background would be appropriate. Because of the meaning of this design, it may be one you'd want to keep for yourself. On the other hand, to give this as a gift would mean you wished the recipient a life of plenty (plenty meaning either material things or wisdom). That would be a very nice gift!

Choose your colors

Besides the factor of what the design calls for, you also want to ensure that the design stands out. A pale pink on white is pretty, but the design will be lost for lack of color contrast. Similarly, if you put medium red on medium green, the design will be lost, and you'll drive your eyes nuts. Choose colors you will enjoy looking at for a long time. If you really dislike blue, for example, it will be difficult to pick up that blue Hawaiian quilt and put in row after row of stitching. Even working with colors you love, give your eyes a break from time to time. It's tiring to look at a high-contrast color scheme, such as red next to white, or orange next to yellow, for a long time. When I worked on my bed-sized 'ULU, which was apple green and light blue, I found that after a while, when I looked up, everything was rosy. Another consideration is whether you want color on white (dark on light) or white on color (light on

dark). I sewed the NAUPAKA design in both red on white and white on red. Color placement can make quite a difference (fig. 2–1).

a.   b.

Fig. 2–1. The same design, in reversed colors. (a) NAUPAKA I (b) NAUPAKA II

Choose your fabric

Generally, traditional Hawaiian quilting is done with 100 percent cotton, solid-colored fabrics. With so many new subtle mottled prints on the market now, you may choose to quilt with one of them. My personal preference is to stick with a solid, because it best emphasizes the graphics of the design.

Buy good quality fabric. You'll see that it's worth it when you align the grain lines of the design piece with the grain lines of the background. You'll appreciate good fabric again when you see how little it frays as you appliqué and how much easier it is to quilt through. Also, better fabrics should mean better quality dyes. I have had problems with some colors, especially medium greens, holding all the dye.

Consider the density of the fabric you choose for your quilt, because you will be quilting through three layers of fabric when quilting the design area. However, if you are putting a white design on a dark background, you may want a denser white fabric, to keep the background color from showing through.

On some of the pieces where I appliquéd a white design on a colored background, I chose an appropriate print for the backing fabric. This adds a nice little surprise when the quilt is turned over, but it also hides all the stitching on the back. If you want to try this, remember to do so only when the background color is medium to dark. Otherwise, the print will show through to the front.

Fabric quantities vary, depending on the width of the fabrics you've chosen. In general, you will need a square at least 42" x 42" up to 45" x 45" for the design, the background, and the backing fabrics. You will need a piece 15" x 42"–45" for the binding and one piece 9" x 39"–42" that matches the backing for the sleeve. See the adjacent tip box for some examples.

Choose your batting

Most of the project quilts were stitched with polyester batting, both medium and low loft. The lower loft batts are better for making small stitches, but medium loft batts will give more definition to your quilting rows. Pā 'Ana a ka Lā and Ahonui were stitched with wool batts, which I found a bit more expensive but easy to work with. Cotton batts will not give enough definition to the *kuiki lau* (echo quilting), but may be appropriate for an historic look with the old style quilting patterns, such as *maka 'upena* (a crisscross grid).

Fabric Fading

Be sure to expose your binding fabric to the same environment as the quilt top while you're working on your quilt. This is more critical with bed-sized quilts, because it can take two or more years to finish the quilt, and you don't want to have different degrees of fading between the top and the binding.

Choose your thread

The oldest Hawaiian quilts were stitched with white thread, because that's all the quilters could get. Using white thread throughout your quilt will lend an historic look to it. Matching thread colors to the area being quilted is perfectly okay. I've been happy with Coats Dual Duty®, for both color selection and thread quality. Dual Duty is cotton covered polyester. Straight uncovered polyester is

How much fabric do I need?

NOTE: We're adding 9" (¼ yard) to all the totals to allow for shrinkage.

Example 1. Let's say you're making a quilt with a dark design on a light background with a light backing. If the dark fabric is 45" wide, you'll need 45" for the design and 15" for the binding. 45"+15"+9"=69", so you'll buy 2 yards (72") of the dark fabric. If the light fabric you chose is also 45" wide, you'll want 45" for the background, plus 45" for the backing, plus 9" for the sleeve. 45"+45"+9"+9"= 108", so you'll buy 3 yards (108") of the light fabric.

Example 2. Now let's switch the colors around. The design will be in a light color on a dark background, with a print backing. Again, we'll say the fabric you like is 45" wide. From the light fabric for the design, you'll need 45"+9"=54". Buy 1½ yards (54") of the light. From the background color, you'll need 45" for the background and 15" for the binding: 45"+15"+9"=69", so buy 2 yards (72") of the dark fabric. From the print backing fabric, you need 45" for the backing and 9" for the sleeve. 45"+9"+9"=63", so buy 1¾ yards (63") of the print.

See yardage chart on page 35.

too strong for cotton fabric. Because I use the smallest size of quilt needle, I have great difficulty threading cotton thread through the needle eye without a threader. I don't like using a threader, so I don't use all-cotton thread. I do not recommend hand-quilting thread, because it is fairly stiff and harder to work with. The new rayon and metallic threads are beautiful, but inappropriate if you want a traditional look.

I cut my wall quilt designs out with standard fabric scissors, but keep a pair of upholstery scissors for cutting out bed quilts. Cutting through eight layers can raise a blister on your thumb, so you may want to bandage up ahead of time.

Gather these additional supplies

To complete your Hawaiian quilt, you will need a few more supplies:

- Very good, sharp fabric scissors
- An 18" hoop
- Hand-appliqué needles (sharps)
- Hand-quilting needles (betweens)
- Good lighting
- A comfortable chair

Using the Patterns

All of the wall quilts shown are 40" x 40", give or take 2". The patterns for them are printed at 50 percent of the full size, to fit on the page. Some of the patterns have been divided to fit on the page. After enlarging the page, join the two segments before tracing the pattern onto your fabric. Trace or photocopy your chosen pattern and have it copied at 200 percent (doubling the size). Businesses listed in the phone book yellow pages as reprographics, blueprinting, or drafting equipment and supplies should be able to do this for you. Don't be shy in asking. They get requests like yours all the time.

If you want to make your quilt larger or smaller than 40" x 40", just calculate the percentage of change you will need and have the pattern copied at that number. For example, if you want to make the quilt 50" x 50", and the pattern will produce a quilt 20" x 20", ask to have the pattern copied at 250 percent. (20" x 250% = 50"). Remember to adjust your fabric requirements accordingly.

Most of the designs are too complex to go smaller than 40" x 40", but the smaller size might work with KALO or PUA MELIA. I made a smaller version of the center of LEI' OKIKA by copying the original 40" pattern at 66 percent and found the elements small enough to make appliqué a challenge.

The quilting pattern *Maka moena* (*lau hala* mat mesh) is shown full size (page 90). Because of the density of this pattern, I suggest using it only for small areas, such as the center of a *lei* design. (see HŌKŪLE'A, on page 46).

To use the overall quilting pattern *Kuiki kuahonu,* (turtle's back), first make nine copies of the full page drawing of the pattern (page 91). Tape those together, matching pattern elements, to make a page three copies across and three down. Take that to the blueprint shop, and ask them to copy it at 200 percent (double the size). That should give you enough of a template to mark a quarter of your quilt at a time. I use a light table and a fine-point silver pencil to trace the pattern onto my quilt top.

Preparing the Materials
Enlarge the pattern

The wall quilt patterns given will need to be enlarged. See Using the Patterns, page 20, for specific directions on how to enlarge them. You can make the pattern any size you want, but if you want to go smaller than 40" x 40", consider the complexity of the design and how easy or difficult it might be to stitch small details. If you want to go larger than 40" x 40", remember that you will have to sew fabric together to get large enough pieces.

Cut the pattern

Carefully cut the paper design along the solid lines with paper scissors. The pattern includes the turn-under allowance. Some patterns require bridges, which temporarily connect sections of the design. Bridges are shown on the pattern as shaded areas (fig. 2–2). Consider them part of the pattern. Bridges help align the design fabric on the background fabric after the design has been cut. AHONUI requires numerous bridges because the design elements are so delicate they can easily be distorted. Treat the bridges just like part of the design until the design fabric is completely basted to the background. Then cut away the bridges so you can do the appliqué.

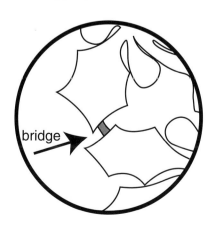

Fig. 2–2. Bridges in the pattern help stabilize delicate areas until the design is basted.

Wash the fabrics

Pre-washing lets you check for dye-fastness and shrinkage. You might be tempted to skip this step if you're making a wallhanging, but spills and stains can occur at any stage of construction, and you would hate to have your quilt shrink or bleed after all the time and effort you put into it. Be sure to iron the fabric before cutting out the design.

Cutting and Basting the Top
Fold the fabric

The traditional way of cutting the design is to fold the fabric into eighths, trace the pattern (which is one-eighth of the total design) onto the top layer, and then cut through all eight layers at once. To properly fold the fabric, you will need a hard, flat surface to work on.

Lay the design fabric flat in front of you. Fold the edge closest to you up to the edge farthest from you. Gently finger-press the fold. Next, fold the right edge over to the left edge. Again, finger-press the fold. Finally, fold the upper-right corner down to the lower-left corner (fig. 2–3).

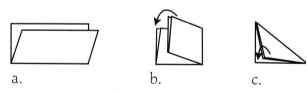

a.   b.   c.

Fig. 2–3. Folding the design fabric. (a) Fold the bottom to the top. (b) Fold the right edge to the left edge. (c) Fold the upper-right corner to the lower-left corner.

Fold Carefully
Follow the instructions to fold your design fabric very carefully. This is important. If the upper-right to lower-left step isn't done correctly, you'll end up with eight little pieces of the design.

Now your fabric is folded into what looks like a triangle. The side of the triangle that is the bias fold should look like one thick fold. Another side of the triangle should be three folds on top of each other. These three folds need to line up perfectly to ensure that identical design elements are cut the same size. The raw edges should all be together on the remaining side of this fabric triangle. Make sure all your folds are neat and match up perfectly, then lightly press with an iron. Do not unfold the fabric just yet.

Place the pattern on the fabric

While the fabric is still folded in eighths, place the pattern on the fabric, matching the side of the pattern marked "bias" (this is usually the longest side of the pattern) to the bias (diagonal) fold of the fabric (fig. 2–4). Match the sides of the pattern to the sides of the fabric, and if there is a center point in the pattern, match it to the folded point of the fabric. If the center of the design is cut out, as in HŌKŪLEʻA, it is important to ensure that the sides of the pattern match the sides of the folded fabric.

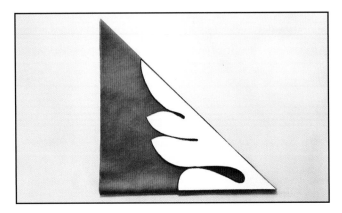

Fig. 2–4. Place the side of the paper pattern marked "bias" on the bias fold of the fabric.

Trace the pattern

Once everything is aligned, pin the pattern to the top layer of fabric and use a pencil to trace around the pattern onto the fabric.

Cut out the design

Remove the pattern and pin all eight layers together, being careful not to shift the layers. Pin outside the design as well as inside. Now, use very sharp scissors to cut slowly and carefully along the pencil line. Do not cut down the folds or you'll end up with eight matching pieces of fabric. Leave the fabric folded after cutting out the design.

Place the design on the background fabric

Fold the background fabric the same way you folded the design fabric. Lightly press the folds, then open the background fabric and spread it flat in front of you. Open the design fabric onto the background fabric and match the fold lines and the centers. Gently smooth the design into place. Make sure that the fold lines and centers are aligned, that there are no ripples in the fabrics, and that the grain lines of the two fabrics are aligned. When the design is laid out smooth and square, pin it down with straight pins. Then, thread baste ¼" inside the design with a light-colored thread (fig. 2–5). If you baste closer to the edge than ¼", you won't have room for the turn-under, and if you baste farther away from the edge, you could end up with the appliqué shifting some as you stitch. Proper basting is essential to a good finished product. For ideas on making work areas for basting, see Basting Surfaces, page 33.

Fig. 2–5. Thread baste the design ¼" inside the edge.

Traditional Hawaiian Appliqué

Begin the appliqué

Hawaiian appliqué is done by simply turning the fabric edge under with a needle as you go. Sew with a turn-under of about ⅛", except at inside points and curves. On the straighter parts of the design, your appliqué stitches should be about ⅛" apart. If they are too close together, it looks like embroidery. If they're too far apart, the design edge may ripple when it is quilted. (Your first row of quilting will be right next to the design.) You will want to put stitches closer together on the curves.

Setting the Mood

Before you settle in to do the appliqué, it's important to set the mood. I love to listen to Hawaiian music as I quilt because it's soothing and puts me in a good frame of mind. If pictures of the beauty of Hawaii help get you motivated, keep some picture books or videos of the islands on hand. Hawaiian quilting is a quiet art, a soothing, relaxing place for good thoughts and meditations. If this quilt is to be a gift, think about the fine qualities of the recipient. Contemplate all your blessings. Thinking good thoughts is an important element in both enjoying the time you will spend with your sewing and in making small, even stitches. You'll be stitching your *mana* (spirit) into this quilt, so you want good, kind, positive thoughts. Put on some Hawaiian music, get a nice cup of tea, and enjoy your appliqué (See the Resources, page 94, if you need sources for Hawaiian music.)

These instructions are for the needle-turn appliqué technique that you will see in probably 99 percent of today's Hawaiian quilts. However, there are a few historical options to consider. Two of these are *humu kā* (cross-stitch), shown in figure 2–6, which I chose when I stitched PUA MELIA, and *wāwae moa* (chicken feet), shown in figure 2–7, which I used for 'ULU. Both of these stitches are fun and fairly easy to do.

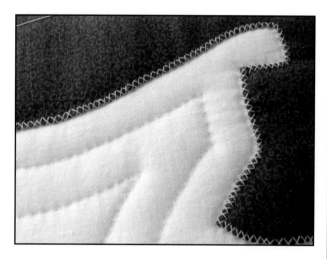

Fig. 2–6. The *humu kā* (cross-stitch) is an historical appliqué stitch.

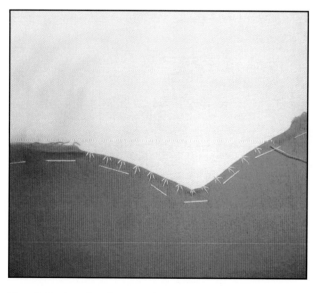

Fig. 2–7. Another historical appliqué stitch is the *wāwae moa* (chicken feet) stitch.

I was taught that the traditional way is to sew along the bottom edge of the design, but I prefer to work along the top edge. Start the appliqué in the middle of a straight area. Using a turn-under allowance of about ⅛", turn under about 1" along the edge of the design fabric. Smooth the edge by sliding the needle under it. Begin the appliqué in the middle of the inch you have turned under (fig. 2–8). Bring your needle up through the background fabric and through about two threads into the design fabric. Then, take the needle straight back down into the background fabric, right next to where it came up.

Travel across the back about ⅛" and bring the needle straight up through the background and the design fabric, again about two threads inside the design fabric (fig. 2–9). Take the needle back down into the background fabric right next to where it came up. Repeat this process all the way around the design.

The stitches on the front of the piece should look like little specks, barely visible and close to the edge of the design (fig. 2–10). The stitches on the back of the piece should look almost like stem stitches. If you are using a light-colored background, be sure to hide all of your thread tails in appliqué stitches on the back, so they don't show through to the front.

Handling curves and points

There's no clipping of curves in traditional Hawaiian appliqué.

Outside curves. On outside curves, just gently and patiently turn under ⅛" and stitch the design down. If you turn under more than ⅛", you'll have a lot of fabric under that curve, just waiting

Fig 2–8. With the needle tip, turn under ⅛" along 1" of the design edge.

Fig. 2–9. Make stitches about ⅛" apart. NOTE: Colored thread is used here for illustration purposes only. Your thread should match the design color..

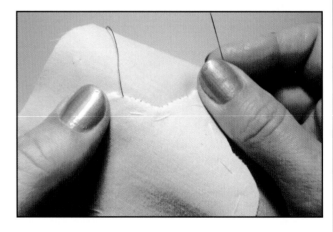

Fig. 2–10. The appliqué stitches should look like tiny specks.

for a chance to make folds and pleats, resulting in pointy curves. If any pleats try to form, smooth them out with your needle, and stitch the curve down.

Inside curves. On inside curves, needle-turn under about ½" ahead of your stitches. You'll see that your turn-under gets pretty narrow. That's okay; you just want a nice, smooth curve. Place your appliqué stitches very close together as you go around the narrow part.

Points. On points, sew to within ⅛" of the tip, turn the tip under with your needle, then turn down ⅛" on the next side of the tip. Take an extra stitch very close to the tip to hold it all in under the point, then continue (fig. 2–11).

Inside Points. Stitching an inside point, or V, is similar to stitching an inside curve. Just stitch down to within ¼" of the V, turn under about ½" ahead of your stitching, form the V with your needle, and stitch it down. There will not be any turn-under at the very point, so your stitches will need to be quite close together to keep threads from popping out later.

Reverse Appliqué. Some designs, such as 'ULU, include reverse appliqué. There's nothing scary here. Just cut the pattern out on all solid lines. Where the design calls for reverse appliqué, this will create "holes" in the design. To reverse appliqué, needle-turn the edge of each hole so the background fabric shows through, and appliqué the edges in place.

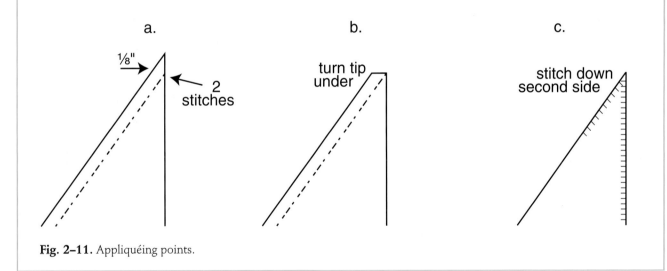

Fig. 2–11. Appliquéing points.

Freezer-Paper Appliqué

The freezer-paper method of appliqué is not traditional in Hawaiian quilting, but if you have arthritis this may be a more comfortable way of cutting out the design. The entire pattern is traced on the design fabric, which is basted, un-cut, onto the background. The design is then cut and appliquéd a small section (about 1" long) at a time instead of being cut all at once.

Supplies

- Paper scissors
- Embroidery scissors
- Pencil or pen for writing on freezer paper
- Freezer paper, at least 42" x 42" square (tape sections together, if necessary)
- Iron
- Fabric marker that will show on your background fabric
- Needle and thread for basting
- Hand-appliqué needles

Fold the freezer-paper square, dull side out, into eighths as shown on page 22. Unfold it and place one diagonal fold line on the bias line of the pattern. Trace the one-eighth pattern on the freezer paper. Refold the freezer paper and cut the design through all eight layers of paper. Unfold the paper template.

freezer paper template

Fold the design fabric into eighths as before. Press and unfold the fabric. Place the freezer paper template on the design fabric, shiny side down. Align the fold lines on the paper and the fabric. Press gently with a warm, dry iron, so the paper sticks to the fabric. With a fabric marker, trace around the freezer-paper template. Don't forget to trace the areas that will be cut out. Peel off the template. Don't cut the design fabric yet.

Place the design fabric square on the background square, right sides up. Referring to the illustration on page 22, thread baste the design fabric square to the background, including basting ¼" inside the design.

The patterns include turn-under allowances, so you will be cutting directly on the drawn pattern line. Be careful to cut only the top (design) fabric.

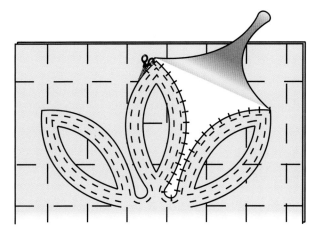

Turn the cut edge of the design fabric under and appliqué in place. Continue in this way, cutting and appliquéing only about 1" at a time.

Preparing for Quilting

Press completed appliqué

Once the appliqué is completed, remove the basting threads and give the piece a good pressing from the back.

NOTE: *Do not* cut the background out from behind the design fabric. Hawaiian quilting is done through all the layers.

Choose a quilting pattern

This is the time to decide if you want to use an overall pattern, such as *Kuiki kuahonu, Kuiki lala, or Pāpa'a pelena,* which are stitched over both the design and the background, or if you want to use *kuiki lau* (echo quilting) in the background and either *kuiki lau* or the flower features in the design area. If you are going to use an overall pattern, mark or trace the quilting pattern now.

Put the layers together

On a smooth, flat surface (see Basting Surfaces, page 33, for ideas), spread the backing fabric out. If you are using a print for the backing, place it right side down. Tape the backing to the smooth surface. I use blue masking tape (painter's tape), available at any hardware store (fig. 2-12).

Next, spread the batting on top of the backing. Make sure it's smooth and even. Finally, place the quilt top on the batting and smooth it out. Usually, quilt instructions will tell you to make the backing a few inches larger than the top, but since you've used the full width of the fabric, your backing and top will be the exact same size (unless you've chosen a different fabric for the backing, in which case the smaller piece of fabric will prevail). Because of this, you will have to be especially careful that the

backing and the top line up perfectly. Double check all the edges for alignment before you start basting. Use a few straight pins to hold everything in place while you baste the three layers together.

Fig. 2–12. Smooth the backing and secure it to a flat surface.

Baste for quilting

Begin basting in the center and sew large stitches to the middle of each edge. Then, stitch parallel rows of basting about every 8", forming a grid pattern. Wherever basting stitches cross the design edge, take the stitches on top, not underneath (fig. 2-13).

Fig. 2–13. Stitch parallel rows of basting every 8" to form a grid pattern

Fig. 2–14. Attach extender strips to each side of the quilt sandwich.

Add extender strips

Prepare your quilt for quilting by adding extender strips. These are strips of scrap fabric, 4" to 6" wide and at least 48" long. They will make it possible for you to quilt all the way to the edge of the quilt in a hoop. While the basted quilt is still taped to the smooth surface, pin the extender strips along the sides of the quilt with straight pins (fig. 2–14). Then machine sew the extender strips on, using a walking foot (even-feed foot) and the largest stitch available. You must use a walking foot, or the layers will shift. If you choose to attach the extender strips by hand, do so while the quilt is still taped to the smooth surface. Sew the strips ⅜" from the edge of the quilt. The binding is going to be ½" wide, so this ⅜" basting will allow room for your quilting to go into the binding area.

Quilting

If you've chosen to use an overall stitch, simply start quilting near the middle of the quilt and gradually work your way toward the edges. Quilt all the way to the edge.

If you've decided to use *kuiki lau* (echo quilting), start by quilting in the background right alongside the design. Quilt all the way around the design, stitching close to the design. If your quilt has a *lei* border, quilt in the background right next to the *lei* border next. Then, you can choose to quilt inside the design first or quilt the background first.

The quilting stitch. Your needle should enter the fabric almost vertically (Fig. 2–15). Then come back up through the fabric, holding the quilt top down with your thumb, just in front of the needle (fig. 2–16, page 30). This stitching method will contribute to the depth of the undulations in the echo quilting.

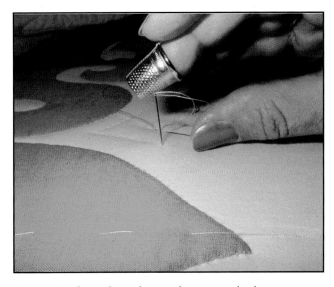

Fig. 2–15. The quilt stitch goes almost straight down into the quilt.

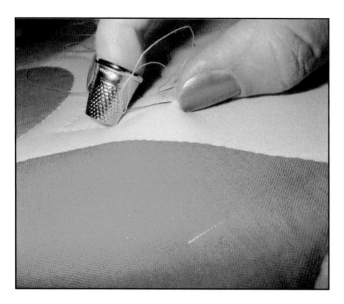

Fig. 2–16. Press down with your thumb on the fabric ahead of the needle.

Quilting the rows. After you've quilted the first row next to the design, place the second row of quilting ½" away from the first and parallel to it. All subsequent rows of quilting should also be ½" apart. For bed-sized quilts, use ⅝" to 1" rows. You can work up to five rows at a time, always stitching the row closest to the design first and working your way to the edge. Trying to do more than five rows will have you moving the hoop too often. Quilt all the way to the edge of the quilt.

Fig. 2–17. After the first row, you can quilt up to five rows at a time.

Blending quilting. If your quilt has a *lei* border, as do PUA MELIA and 'ULU, stitch along the edge of the *lei* in the background, right next to the *lei*, just as you did with the design. Then blend the echo quilting coming out from the center design with the echo quilting coming in from the *lei*. I suggest doing equal numbers of rows from each direction until they meet. Look closely at the design area in HŌKŪLE'A to see how to merge the rows of quilting.

Finishing the Quilt

Trim the edges

Once you've finished your quilting, take off the extender strips and square up the edges. If the fabric pieces were square when you started out and you were careful setting up the basting before quilting, there should be little or no trimming to do. If you do need to trim, be sure to not cut into your quilting, or you'll have to re-knot a lot of threads. This is the time to make sure the quilt is square.

Attach the binding

I prefer ½" wide bindings for my Hawaiian quilts. It looks more like the historical quilts, and a colored binding around a white background creates a nice frame for the quilt. The method I use involves putting the binding on each side separately, and requires that the binding strips be at least 1" longer than the quilt. If you don't have long enough binding strips, you may choose to piece together five binding strips and apply with mitered corners.

Binding method. Cut four strips 3" x 43"–46" (3" x the width of the binding fabric). Fold these 3" strips in half lengthwise and press. Lay the quilt out flat on a hard surface, design side up. For the left and right sides, measure the quilt down the center from the top edge to the bottom edge. Cut the two side binding strips to that measurement. Match the raw edges of the folded binding strips with the raw edges of the quilt. Carefully pin the binding strips to the side edges, on the design side (front) of the quilt, easing as needed to make the binding strips match the edges of the quilt (fig. 2-18). Make certain there are no ripples or pleats under the binding or on the back. Machine stitch, using a walking foot (even-feed foot) ½" from the raw edges. Bring the binding strips over the edge of the quilt and hand sew to the back of quilt. (Choose a thread the same color as the binding and sew with the same stitch described earlier for appliqué).

For the top and bottom edges, lay two binding strips across the middle of the quilt, from side to side, and extending past the side binding. Use pins to mark the width of the quilt on the binding (fig. 2–19). Leave ½" to 1" at the ends of the strips. Do not remove the pins. Position the binding strips along the top and bottom edges of the quilt, matching the raw edges and aligning the pins with the sides of the quilt. Pin the strips to the quilt and machine stitch ½" from the raw edges. Remember to leave that extra ½" to 1" extending beyond the ends.

a.

Fig. 2–19. Place the top and bottom binding strips across the middle of the quilt and use pins to mark where they meet the bound side edges.

To finish the ends of the top and bottom edge bindings, fold the binding back on itself so the folded edge meets the seam line. Then stitch across the ends (fig. 2–20). Trim the ends to about ⅛", turn the binding back over the quilt edge, and hand stitch the binding to the back of the quilt, just as you did on the first two sides.

Fig. 2–18. Binding the side edges. (a) Measure the quilt from top to bottom, across the center. (b) Cut two binding strips to size, match the raw edges, pin, and sew.

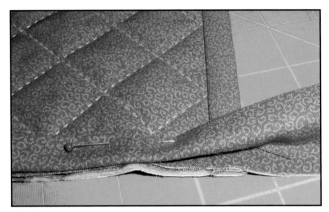

a.

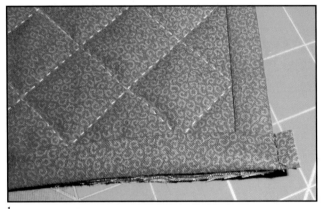

b.

Fig. 2–20. (a) Fold the binding back on itself.
(b) Stitch across the ends.

Add the sleeve

Most quilt shows and competitions call for a 4" wide sleeve, so just make it a habit to always use a 4" sleeve. To make the sleeve, cut a piece of fabric that matches the backing to 9" x 39". Turn the shorter sides under ¼" and hem them. Then fold the piece in half lengthwise, *wrong sides together,* and stitch a ¼" seam down the long side. Refold the sleeve lengthwise so that the seam is in the center of one side and press. Hand stitch the sleeve (with the seam side against the quilt) to the top of the back of the quilt, sewing down the long sides of the sleeve. At the ends of the sleeve, stitch the part of the sleeve touching the quilt backing to the quilt back. This will keep the hanging rod from slipping between the sleeve and the quilt.

Fig. 2–21. With the seam against the back of the quilt, hand sew the sleeve in place.

Attach your label

After all the effort you've put into making your beautiful Hawaiian-style quilt, be sure to put a label on it. At the very least, give the quilt's name, your name, and the date the quilt was completed. You may also want to state on the label the purpose of the quilt, such as a remembrance of a special date or a gift to someone dear. If the quilt is a gift, add care instructions.

Last step! Pau!

Once the quilt is completed, give it a little pat, declaring it *pau* (finished). This last step is a Hawaiian ritual. If you've made a full-sized bed quilt, you must sleep under it one night to get back out of the quilt enough *mana* to continue making Hawaiian quilts. If you've made a wall quilt, I think a hug would do. Then silently give thanks for having the time and talent to make such a beautiful piece, and thank the quilt for giving you so much pleasure.

Basting Surfaces

Making an inexpensive basting table

A suitable basting surface must be smooth, hard, and high enough for you. (I'm 5'7" and have my basting table at 34½", the same as my cutting table.) The proper height will reduce the strain on your back and legs. Ideally, you need room, at least temporarily, to set up the table where you can walk all the way around it. This will make the basting easier and more comfortable.

To make the basting table, go to a home improvement store with a friend who has a truck or mini-van and get a 4' x 8' piece of particle board covered with laminate. Have the store clerk cut it in half, and you and your friend will each get a tabletop 4'x4'. You can also purchase laminate edge tape that you can iron onto the sides of your table at home.

If you have room to keep the table set up, just add legs long enough to get the right height for comfortable basting and cutting. For a temporary or convertible setup, use a card table or similar piece of furniture as a base and add wood chocks or encyclopedia volumes to raise the table to a comfortable height. I use four 2-shelf bookcases arranged in a square for my base. The bookcases make the tabletop just the right height to use as an extension for my sewing machine cabinet. For basting, I just use four encyclopedia volumes under each end of the tabletop. I can't walk all the way around the table with it butted up against the sewing machine cabinet, but otherwise it works great.

Making a basting surface on the floor

If your home, like mine, is carpeted throughout, you may not have a place on the floor to baste larger quilts. The remedy involves another trip to the home improvement store. Purchase up to three 4' x 8' sheets of smooth, glossy white paneling, depending on the size of the quilts you plan to baste. A queen-sized quilt, for example, requires all three panels, while a wall quilt may only need one. These panels are light and fairly easy to maneuver. Simply lay them over the carpeting to do your basting. By using the panels, you won't have to reach across a table to baste; just sit on the quilt as you work. Blue painter's masking tape can hold the quilt backing in place without damaging the panel, and the panels can be stored in the garage.

My table normally looks like this and works as an extension of my sewing machine cabinet.

This is the same table with encyclopedia volumes boosting it to a comfortable height for basting.

Chapter Three: Patterns – Wall Quilts

Use the following yardage chart for all of the quilts. Trace or photocopy your chosen pattern, take it to a blueprint or drafting supplies shop, and have it copied at 200 percent. General instructions for making Hawaiian quilts begin on page 17.

Yardage for 40" Wall Quilts

NOTE: These measurements include an extra quarter yard to allow for shrinkage or possible miscutting at the store.

When using a dark design on a light background

Fabric#1	**Yardage**	**Cut pieces**
Design	2	one square at least 42" x 42"
& Binding		five 3" wide strips, cut selvage to selvage

Fabric#2	**Yardage**	**Cut pieces**
Background	3	one square at least 42" x 42"
& Backing		one square at least 42" x 42"
& Sleeve		one strip 9" x 39"

When using a light design on a dark background

Fabric#1	**Yardage**	**Cut pieces**
Design	1½	one square at least 42" x 42"

Fabric#2	**Yardage**	**Cut pieces**
Background	3½	one square at least 42" x 42"
& Backing		one square at least 42" x 42"
& Sleeve		one strip 9" x 39"
& Binding		five 3" wide strips, cut selvage to selvage

When using a light design, dark background, and print backing

Fabric#1	**Yardage**	**Cut pieces**
Design	1½	one square at least 42" x 42"

Fabric#2	**Yardage**	**Cut pieces**
Background	2	one square at least 42" x 42"
& Backing		five 3" wide strips, cut selvage to selvage

Fabric#3	**Yardage**	**Cut pieces**
Background	1¾	one square at least 42" x 42"
& Sleeve		one strip 9" x 39"

Pua Melia
Plumeria

Pua Melia is a simple design, easy to complete. Plumeria is one of my favorite flowers, with delicate, fragrant blossoms. I appliquéd this design with *humu kā* (cross-stitch). The stitch is not difficult, but keeping the stitches all the same size can be a bit challenging. Mine ended up averaging ten stitches per inch. *Humu kā* is an old stitch, most often seen on the center square of *kapa hae* (flag quilts).

Pua Melia (Plumeria), 40" x 40", by the author. A very small, monochromatic print was used for the blue fabric. This was done in the old days, but since busy prints can hide all your beautiful quilting, be very selective about print fabrics. I chose one of the old *i'e kuku* patterns, *kuiki maka 'upena*, for the *lei*.

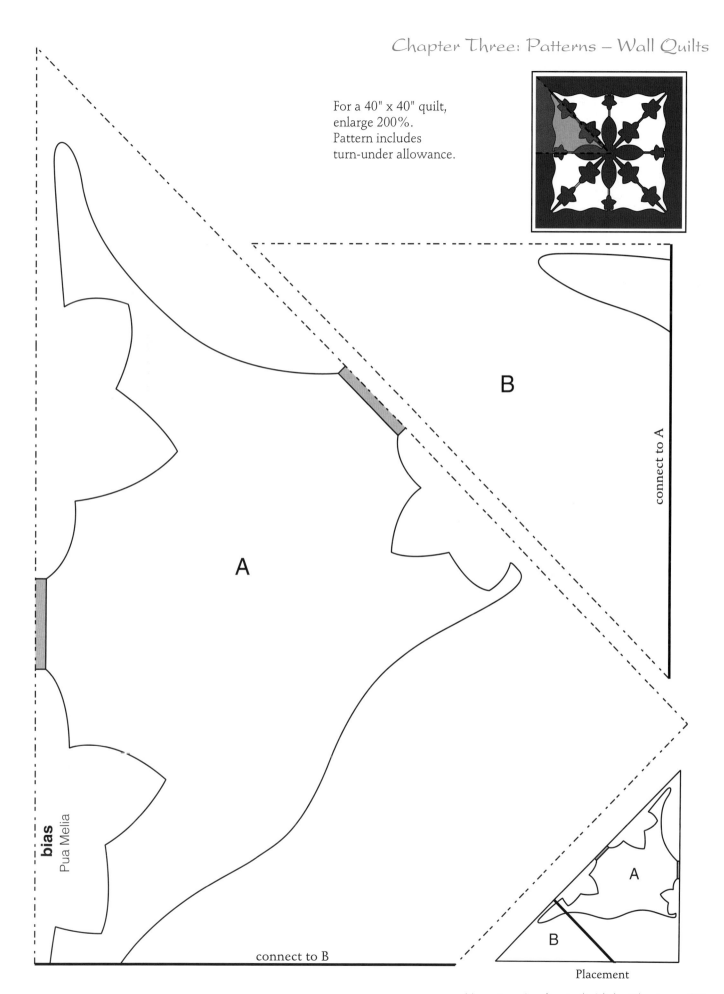

For a 40" x 40" quilt,
enlarge 200%.
Pattern includes
turn-under allowance.

B

connect to A

A

bias
Pua Melia

connect to B

A

B

Placement

HALA KAHIKI
Pineapple

HALA KAHIKI is a simple design, quickly appliquéd. Shown here with the *Kuiki kuahonu*, or turtle's back, quilting pattern, this design would also look great done with *kuiki lau* (echo quilting) in the background and a crosshatch or scalloped design within the pineapples to show the texture of the fruit.

HALA KAHIKI (Pineapple), 40" x 40", by the author. The *Kuiki kuahonu*, or turtle's back, quilting pattern originated on Kaua'i. The earliest example I found was made in 1904. The turtle's back pattern is sometimes also called *honu ipu*.

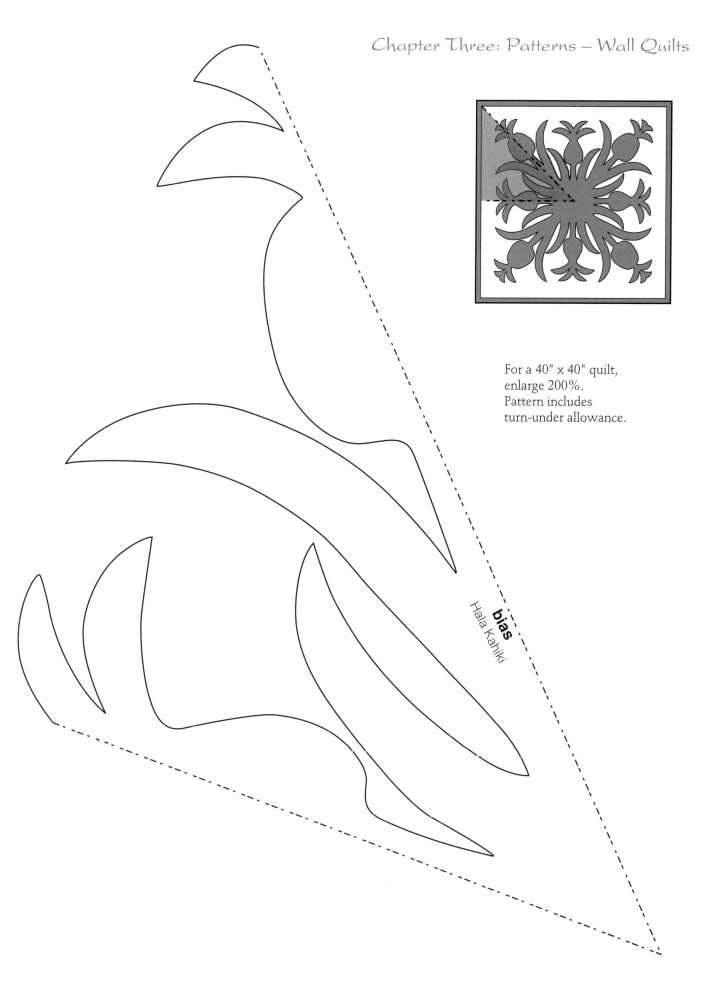

For a 40" x 40" quilt,
enlarge 200%.
Pattern includes
turn-under allowance.

bias
Hala Kahiki

KALO

Taro

Taro represents our kinship with all of nature. Taro was the first-born of Earth Mother and Sky Father, with the first human sibling born later. Taro is a medicinal plant and is the source of *poi*, an important starch food in the early Hawaiian diet.

KALO (Taro), 40" x 40", by the author. This quilt, of all my designs, best represents the native, traditional way of life. It is green, the color of taro, on white 100 percent cotton, with white backing and green ½" binding. It is quilted *kuiki lau*, except for the taro leaf detail.

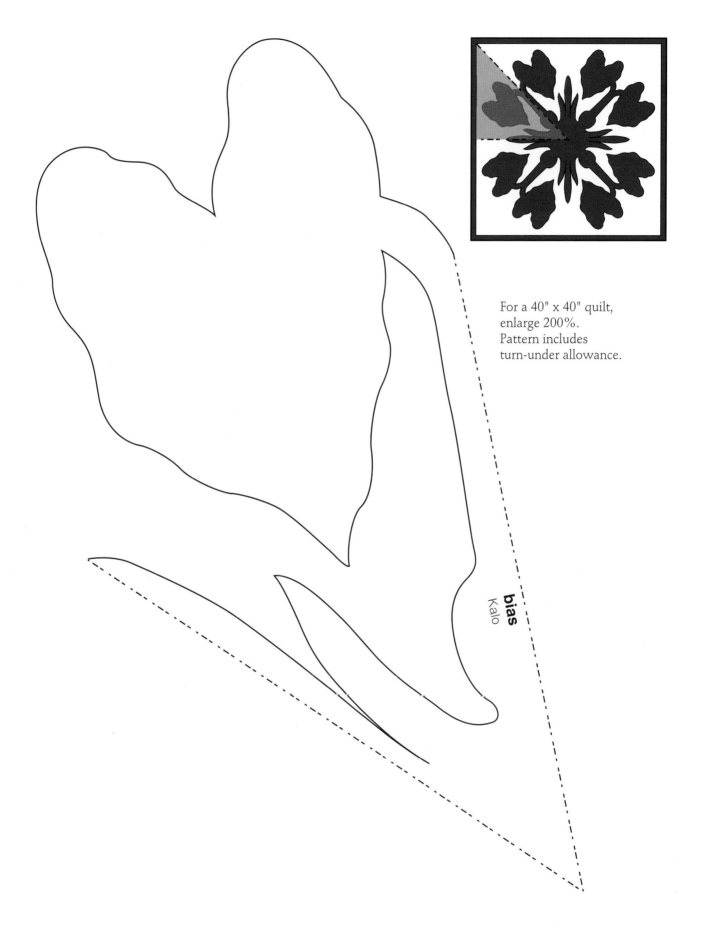

For a 40" x 40" quilt,
enlarge 200%.
Pattern includes
turn-under allowance.

bias
Kalo

'ULU

Breadfruit

This design has a simple center element and a *lei* border. Within the border, the '*Ulu* design is done with reverse appliqué. Refer to the instructions in Chapter Two, page 25, for reverse appliqué.

'ULU (Breadfruit), 40" x 40", by the author. While '*ulu* means breadfruit, *ulu* means to grow in wisdom and to never hunger. The two meanings are mingled in quilting, so that to make 'ULU your first quilt means that you will never hunger and will grow in wisdom, and that you will continue to make quilts.

Placement

For a 40" x 40" quilt,
enlarge 200%.
Pattern includes
turn-under allowance.

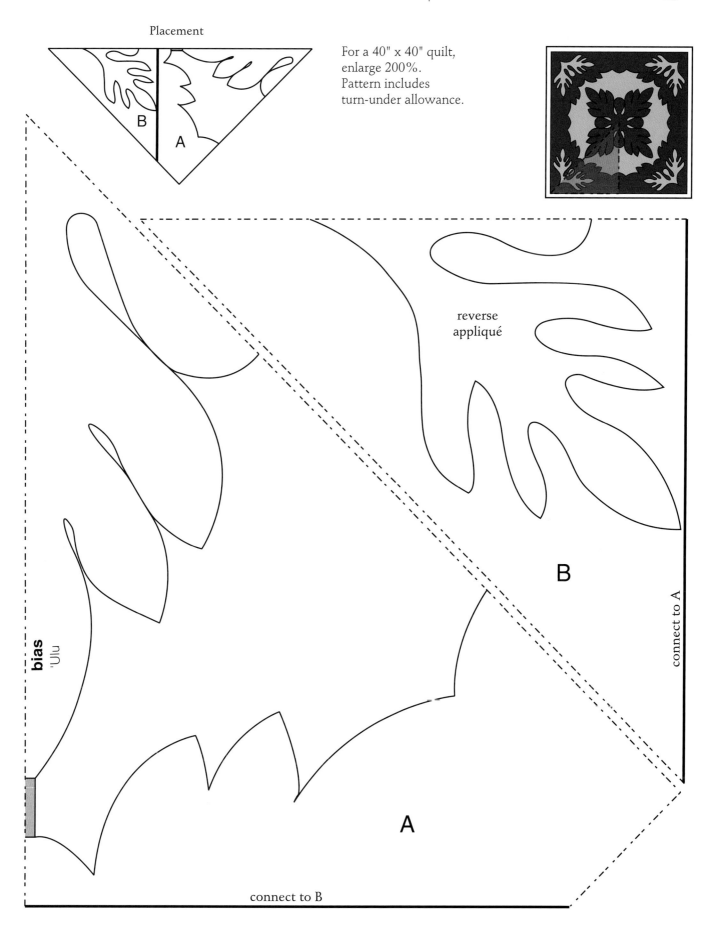

reverse
appliqué

bias
'Ulu

B

connect to A

A

connect to B

Nā Pua Ulu Pono Me Aloha

Children Thrive with Love

This is an example of using two colors, rather than white and one color. The green is a softly mottled print, which looks rather lush. I had plumeria blossoms in mind when I chose the pink color. This design would also be striking in red on white.

Nā Pua Ulu Pono Me Aloha (Children Thrive with Love), 40" x 40", by the author. I chose this title to remind viewers that children, like flowers (*pua* means both flower and offspring) thrive with love and attention.

For a 40" x 40" quilt,
enlarge 200%.
Pattern includes
turn-under allowance.

bias

Nā Pua Ulu Pono Me Aloha

HŌKŪLE'A

Hōkūle'a means happy star and is the Hawaiian name for Arcturus. This star is important in navigating to Hawaii because it passes directly overhead of the islands. *Hōkūle'a* is also the name of a Polynesian voyaging canoe built in 1973–1975 in Hawaii and used to prove that navigating between the islands of Polynesia without modern instruments was possible. The voyages of *Hōkūle'a* sparked a cultural renaissance throughout the South Pacific which continues to this day. To read more about this voyaging canoe, check out www.pvs-hawaii.org.

HŌKŪLE'A, 40" x 40", by the author. This quilt design honors the voyaging canoe Hōkūle'a and everyone who worked on it. The center of the quilt is stitched with the *Maka moena,* or lau hala mat, pattern. The sails are quilted with curving parallel lines to illustrate the seams of the sails. The background is quilted *kuiki lau,* (echo quilting) with a thread one shade darker than the fabric.

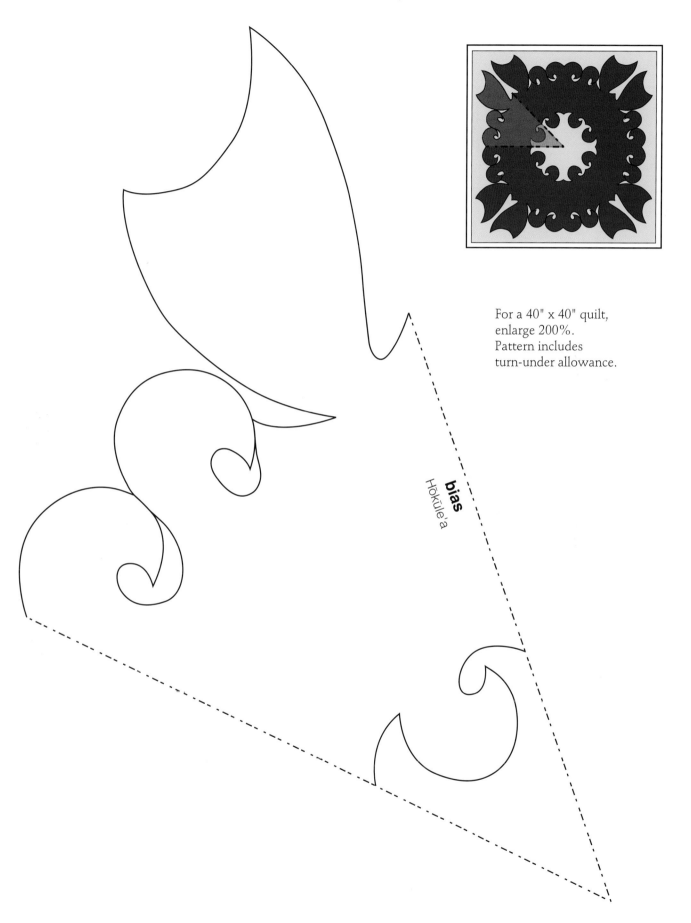

For a 40" x 40" quilt,
enlarge 200%.
Pattern includes
turn-under allowance.

bias
Hōkūle'a

AMAZON LILY

This is one of the first Hawaiian-style quilts I designed, and it's still one of my very favorites. The Amazon lily is a beautiful white flower with large dark green leaves.

AMAZON LILY, 40" x 40", by the author. Made of 100 percent cotton, with a polyester batt. This piece is quilted *kuiki lau* (echo quilting) except for the flowers.

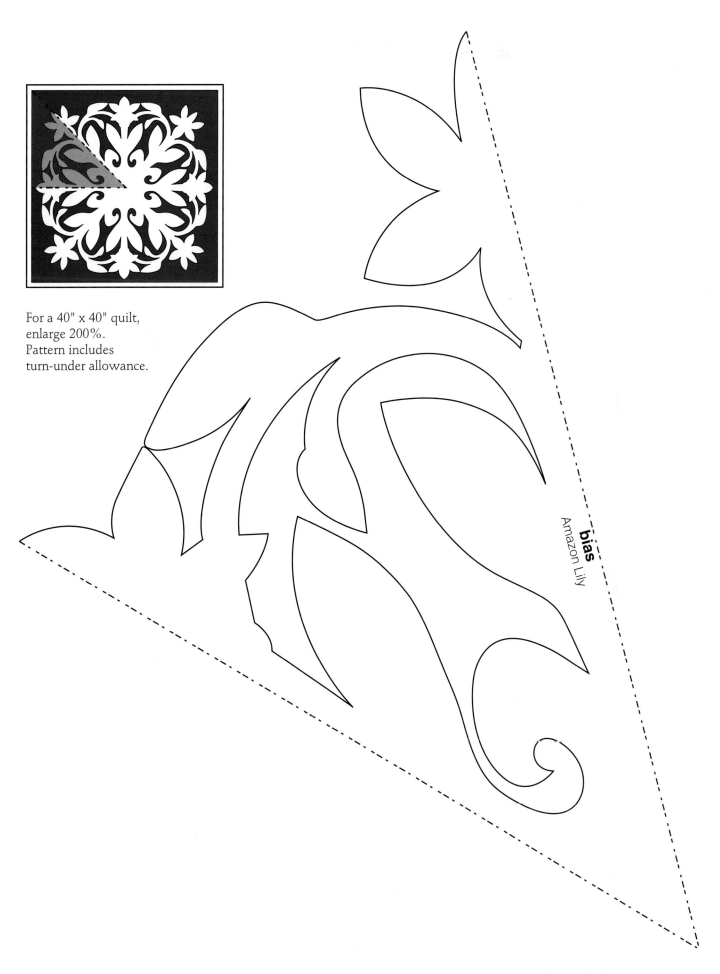

For a 40" x 40" quilt,
enlarge 200%.
Pattern includes
turn-under allowance.

bias
Amazon Lily

Naupaka

Naupaka is a shrub with small white half-flowers, which represent lovers (once a whole flower) forever torn apart. One was banished to the mountain and the other to the seashore. The mountain naupaka blossom has pointed petals, while the seashore blossoms are rounded.

NAUPAKA 40" x 40", by the author. I liked this design so much, I did it twice. The white on red has a print backing. The red on white has a white backing and red ½" wide binding. Both quilts are made of 100 percent cotton with polyester batting and are quilted with the very traditional *kuiki lau* (echo quilting) design. The quilts were quilted with threads matching the fabric colors.

For a 40" x 40" quilt,
enlarge 200%.
Pattern includes
turn-under allowance.

Placement

connect to A

B

A

bias
Naupaka

connect to B

PEACEFUL VALLEY

At the time I designed PEACEFUL VALLEY, I was unaware of the *kapu* against combining different plants on the same stems. That's because they don't grow that way in nature. I wanted a quilt that would convey a Garden of Eden type lushness and profusion of foliage.

PEACEFUL VALLEY, 40" x 40", by the author. Anthuriums, lilies, orchids, and plumeria are in this quilt, which is quilted totally *kuiki lau* (echo quilting). It is made of 100 percent cotton, with a polyester batt.

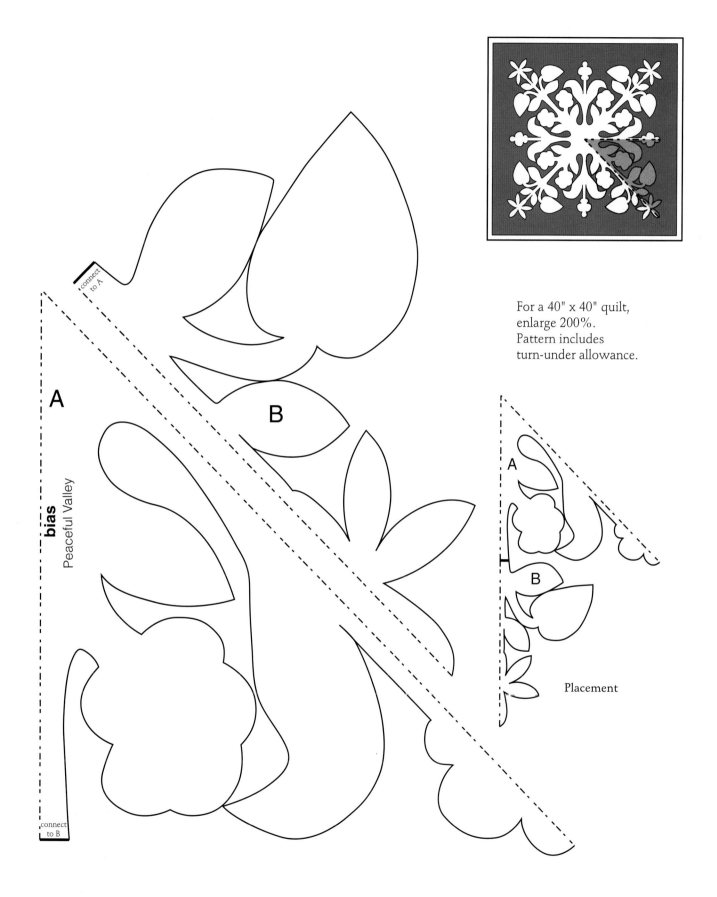

For a 40" x 40" quilt,
enlarge 200%.
Pattern includes
turn-under allowance.

A
bias
Peaceful Valley

connect to A

connect to B

B

A

B

Placement

PĀ 'ANA A KA LĀ

Sunshine

The quilting pattern on this quilt is *Kuiki lala*, diagonal lines. It's an old style quilting pattern, sometimes shown with two or three parallel lines about ½" apart, then a space of ¾" to 1", then two or three lines again. I choose to stitch single diagonal rows ½" apart. The batting is machine washable wool. This design would also look great with the flowers quilted like orchids and the background echo quilted. The *Kuiki kuahonu* (turtle's back) quilting pattern would also look wonderful on this design.

Pā 'Ana A Ka Lā (Sunshine), 40" x 40", by the author. This piece started out a bright lemon yellow, but it wouldn't photograph well. So after it was all finished, I tea-dyed it. That not only makes it show up better, it also makes it look older. After the tea-dying, I pressed the quilt to give it a "been in the museum a long time" look.

For a 40" x 40" quilt,
enlarge 200%.
Pattern includes
turn-under allowance.

bias
Pā'Ana A Ka Lā

ALOALO

Hibiscus

This design took longer to appliqué because of all the little notches on the leaves. If you are new to Hawaiian quilting, or if you want a simpler project, you may want to make the leaf edges smooth for easier appliqué.

ALOALO (Hibiscus), 40" x 40", by the author. This quilt was sewn with 100 percent cotton fabrics and a polyester batt. The background is quilted *kuiki lau* (echo quilting), and the flowers' features are shown with quilting.

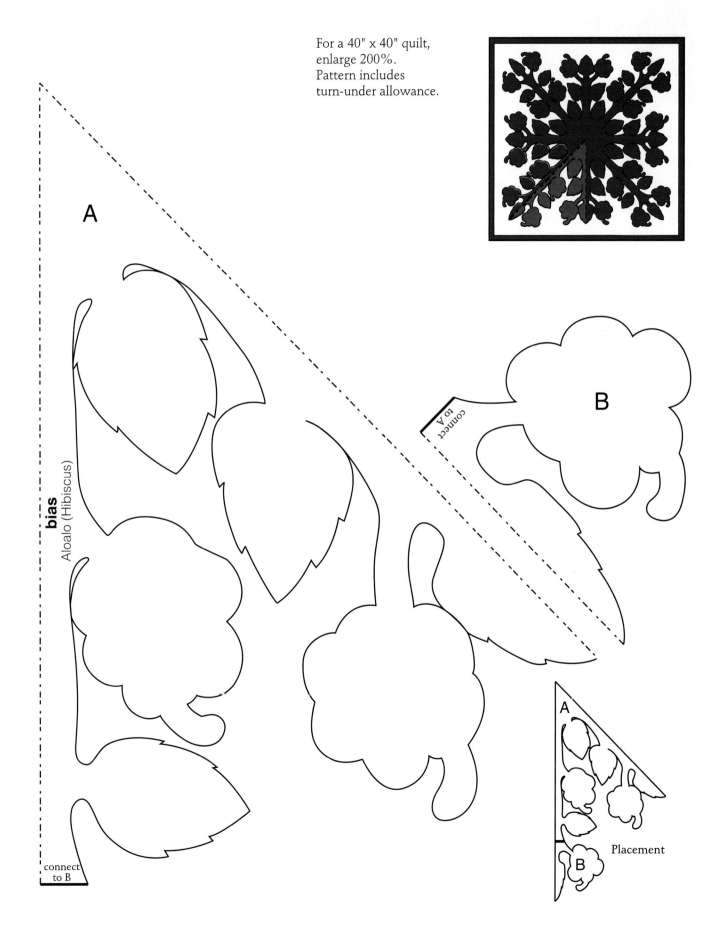

For a 40" x 40" quilt,
enlarge 200%.
Pattern includes
turn-under allowance.

A

bias
Aloalo (Hibiscus)

connect
to A

B

A

B

Placement

connect
to B

MIDNIGHT IN WAIMANALO
The Gossip Quilt

This design is meant to depict the orchids in a Waimanalo, O'ahu greenhouse, leaning toward each other to catch every last bit of gossip when it's midnight and no humans are around to hear them. It's also hoped that this title will be a reminder to keep our gossip kind.

MIDNIGHT IN WAIMANALO (The Gossip Quilt), 40" x 40", by the author. Two visits to an orchid vendor from Waimanalo, O'ahu, at an orchid show in Miami were the inspiration for this design. The orchid model was a pansy miltonia. The mottled background fabric looked like a midnight sky to me.

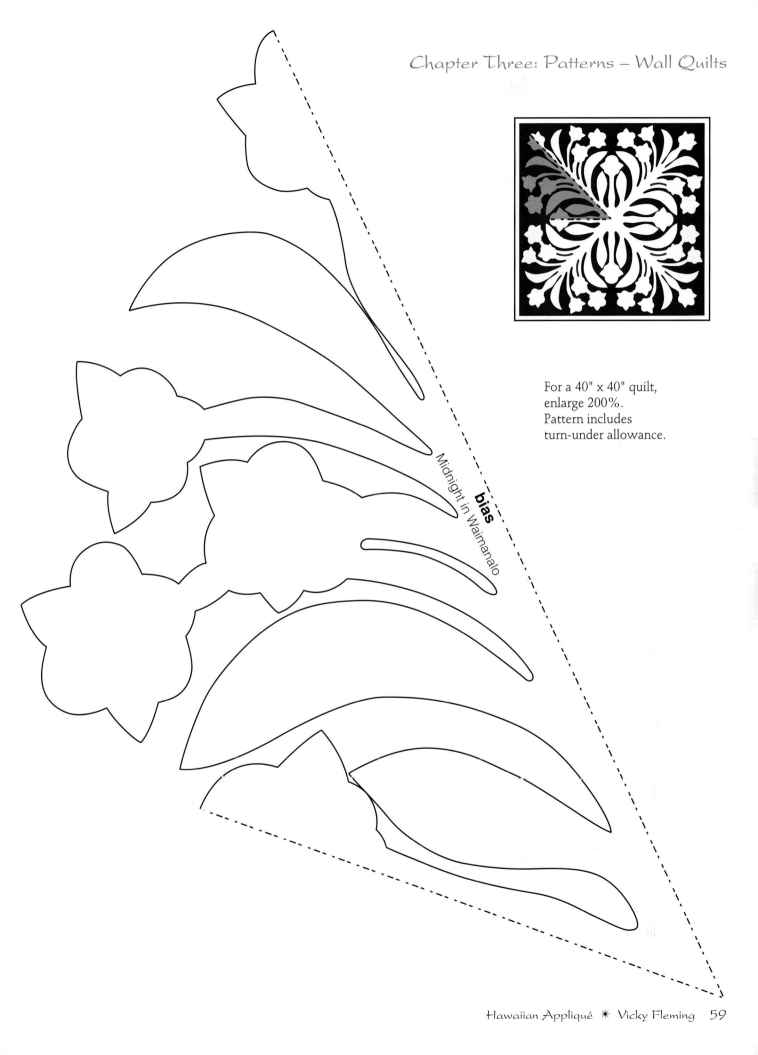

bias

Midnight in Waimanalo

For a 40" x 40" quilt,
enlarge 200%.
Pattern includes
turn-under allowance.

Lei 'Okika

Orchid Lei

The quilting on Lei 'okika is *kuiki lau* (echo quilting), except for the flowers and leaves. I started out with just the center, and was well into the quilting before I decided the design just had to have corners. It would have been *much* easier to position and appliqué the corners *before* the quilt top was layered with batting and backing!

Lei 'okika (Orchid Lei), 40" x 40", by the author. Made from 100 percent cotton with a polyester batt. The backing is a multi-colored print.

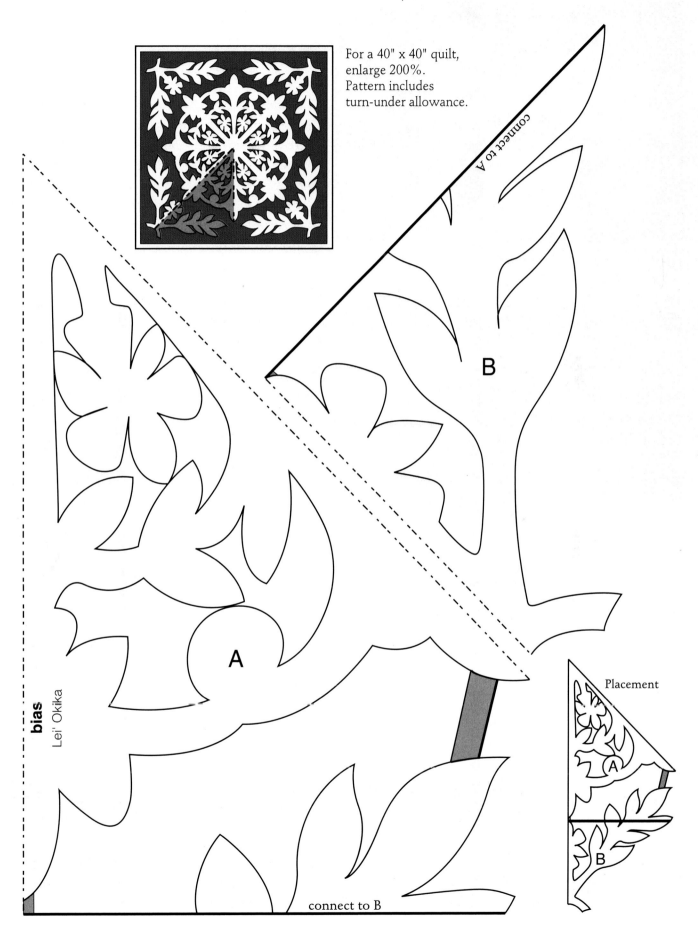

For a 40" x 40" quilt, enlarge 200%. Pattern includes turn-under allowance.

connect to A

B

bias

Lei' Okika

A

Placement

A

B

connect to B

PĀ LILIA

Lily Fence

I had seen a wrought iron fence around a church in Hawaii, and wanted to do something with the fence design. The popular, pre-1933 design KA LANAI O KOLOMONA (Solomon's Porch) was also part of the inspiration for PĀ LILIA. The design looks something like a fleur-de-lis, so that's how the name came to be Lily Fence.

PĀ LILIA (LILY FENCE), 40" x 40", by the author. This quilt has a print backing and a polyester batt. It's quilted *kuiki lau* (echo quilting), with a fair amount of reverse appliqué.

Placement

bias
Pā Lilia

A

connect to B

connect to A

B

For a 40" x 40" quilt,
enlarge 200%.
Pattern includes
turn-under allowance.

WINDS OF CHANGE

This the most personal of my Hawaiian-style quilts. On Mother's Day in 1989, with a wonderful thunderstorm on the way, my step-daughter called to say she was expecting her first child. As I digested this news, I watched some bamboo-like trees swaying in the wind. Those trees are reflected in this design.

WINDS OF CHANGE, 40" x 40", by the author. The original design went right to the edge of the 45" fabric, so I have reproduced the pattern a little bit smaller to allow for a few rows of quilting. WINDS OF CHANGE is quilted *kuiki lau* (echo quilting), except for the flowers.

For a 40" x 40" quilt, enlarge 200%. Pattern includes turn-under allowance.

Placement

B

A

connect to B

bias
Winds of Change

A

A

B

connect to A

AHONUI

Patience

I love the slender, curvy elements of this design, but I would not recommend it for beginning quilters because of the challenge in getting it laid out evenly and the time it takes to appliqué.

AHONUI (PATIENCE), 40" x 40", by the author. The quilt is 100 percent cotton with a wool batt. The design would also look great in green on either white or pink as a holiday quilt, because the leaves look rather like holly leaves.

For a 40" x 40" quilt,
enlarge 200%.
Pattern includes
turn-under allowance.

bias
Ahonui

Pillow Patterns

These ten patterns, printed full-size, are for 20" blocks. Use them individually as pillow tops, add a border to make a wall quilt, or piece several of the blocks together, with or without sashing, to make a *kapa pohopoho* (patchwork quilt).

For each of the blocks, you will need a 20" square for the design and a 20" square for the background. How you decide to use the blocks will determine which other fabrics you might need.

Pineapple (p. 69)

Mālama Hawai'i (p. 70)

Naupaka (p. 71)

Hibiscus (p. 72)

Coconut Palm (p. 73)

Plumeria (p. 74)

'Ōhi'a Lehua (p. 75)

Orchid (p. 76)

'Ulu (p. 77)

Ti Leaf (p. 78)

Bonus Wall Quilt

Tahitian Bouquet (p. 79)

Pineapple

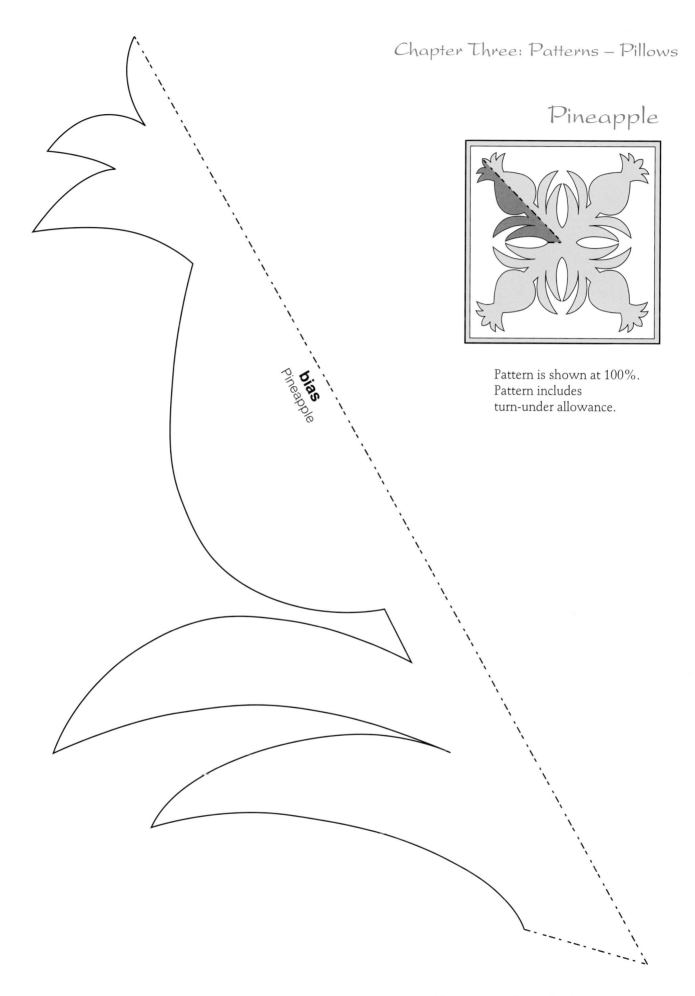

bias
Pineapple

Pattern is shown at 100%.
Pattern includes
turn-under allowance.

Mālama Hawai'i
(Take care of Hawai'i)

Pattern is shown at 100%.
Pattern includes
turn-under allowance.

Mālama Hawai'i
bias

Naupaka

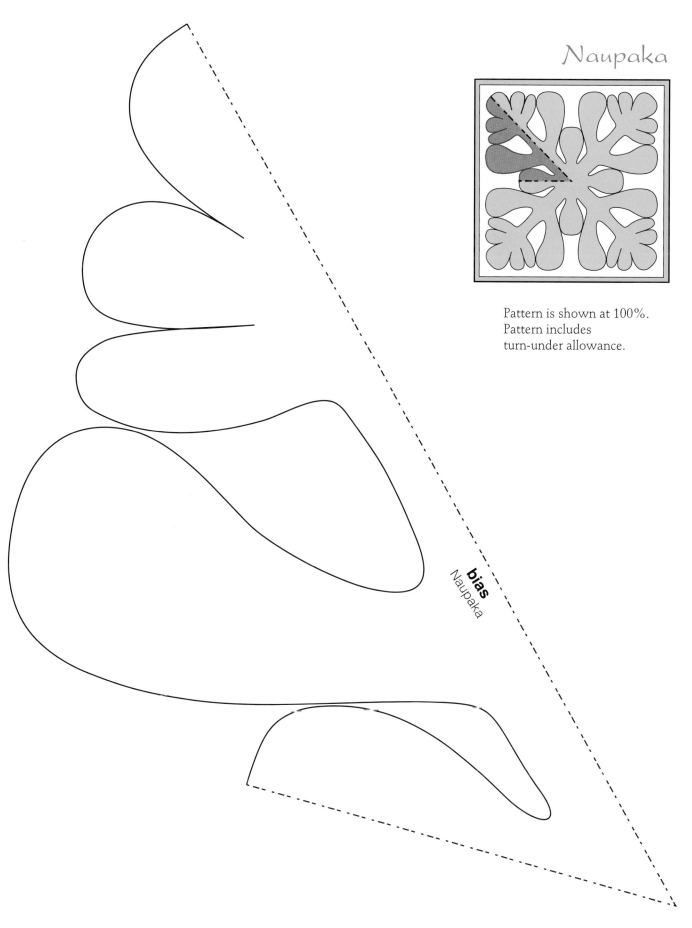

Pattern is shown at 100%.
Pattern includes
turn-under allowance.

bias
Naupaka

Hibiscus

Pattern is shown at 100%.
Pattern includes
turn-under allowance.

bias
Hibiscus

Coconut Palm

Pattern is shown at 100%.
Pattern includes
turn-under allowance.

bias
Coconut Palm

Plumeria

bias
Plumeria

Pattern is shown at 100%.
Pattern includes
turn-under allowance.

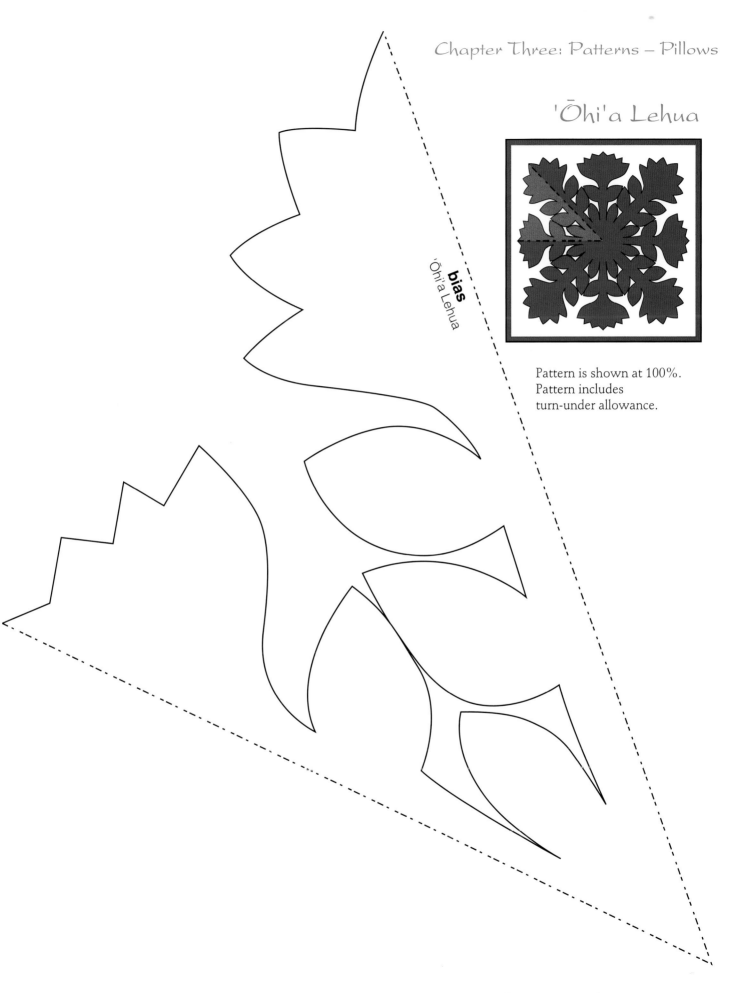

'Ōhi'a Lehua

bias
'Ōhi'a Lehua

Pattern is shown at 100%.
Pattern includes
turn-under allowance.

Orchid

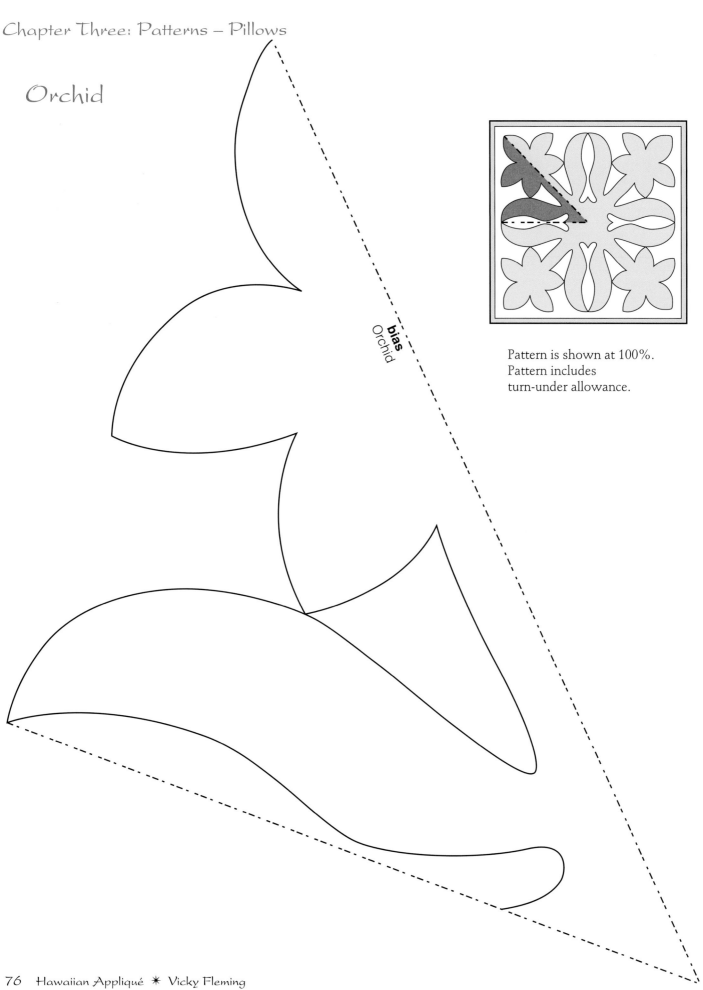

bias
Orchid

Pattern is shown at 100%.
Pattern includes
turn-under allowance.

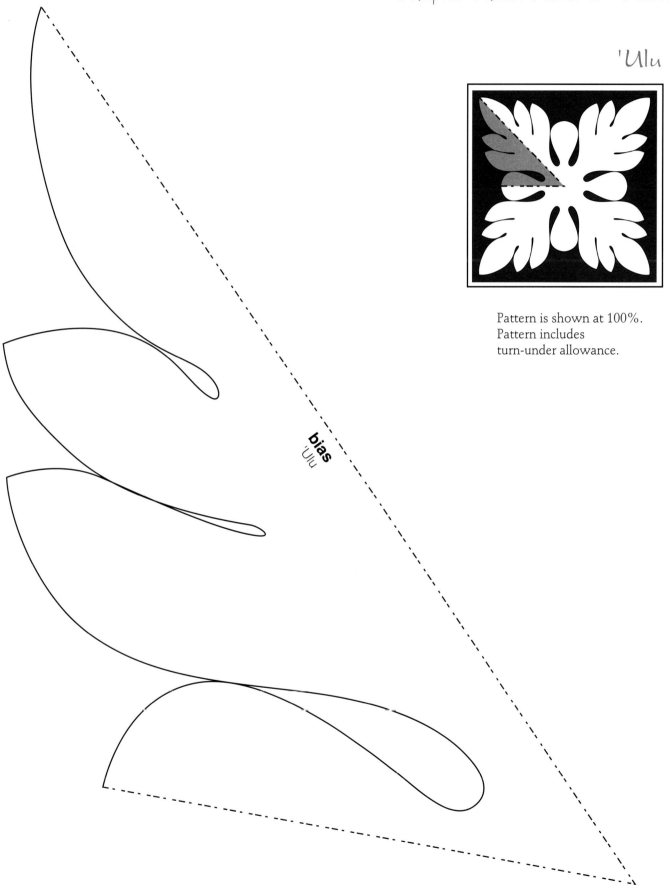

'Ulu

bias
'Ulu

Pattern is shown at 100%.
Pattern includes
turn-under allowance.

Ti Leaf

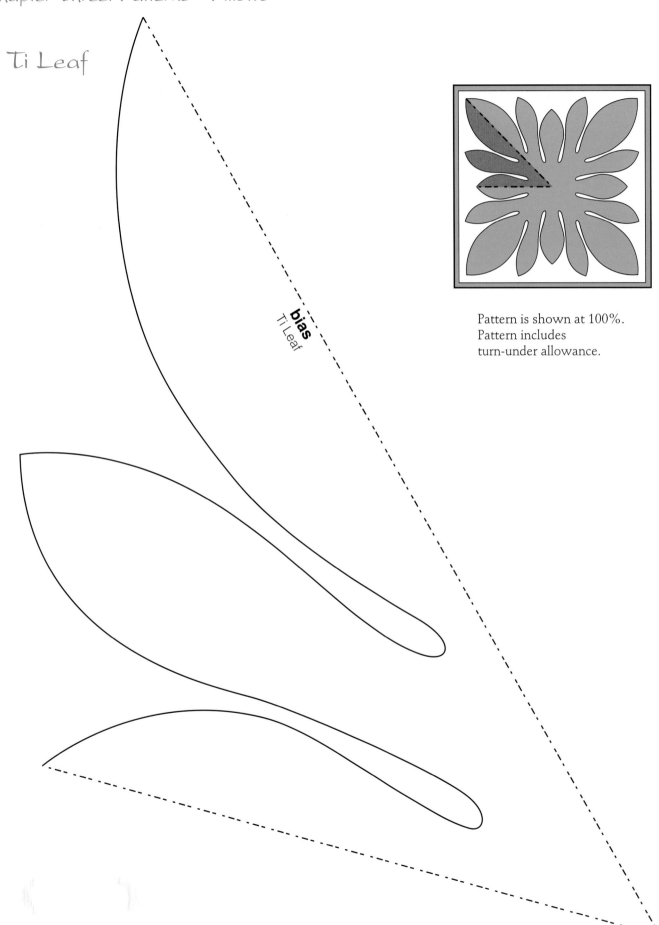

bias
Ti Leaf

Pattern is shown at 100%.
Pattern includes
turn-under allowance.

Bonus Wall Quilt

Tahitian Bouquet

bias
Tahitian
Bouquet

connect to B

A

Placement

B A

This design is more like the Tahitian *tifaifai* (quilt), which is usually quarter-folded, then appliquéd in the same manner as Hawaiian quilts. They do not have batting, and they are not quilted, simply backed.

This pattern, enlarged 250 percent, will create a wall quilt 47" x 47". You will need 2⅞ yards each for the background, design fabric, and backing. After washing and ironing the fabric, cut each piece into two 48" lengths and seam them together. Trim each 48" x 96" piece to 48" x 48", reserving the remaining fabric for the binding and sleeve.

Tahitian Bouquet

For a 47" x 47" quilt, enlarge 250%.
Pattern includes
turn-under allowance.
Connect to A on page 79.

Placement

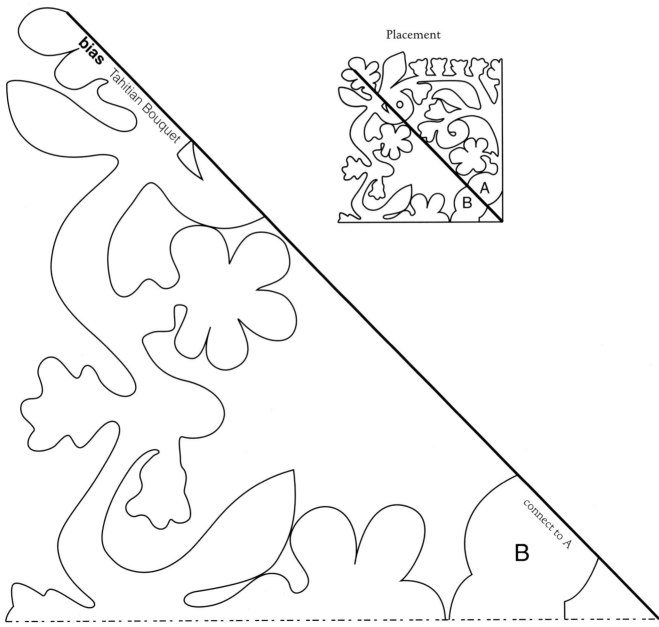

bias

Tahitian Bouquet

connect to A

B

Ha'ao (p. 82)

Iwi-puhi (p. 83)

Chapter Four: Beyond Echo Quilting

Iwi-puhi, II (p. 84)

Hālu'a 'upena (p. 85)

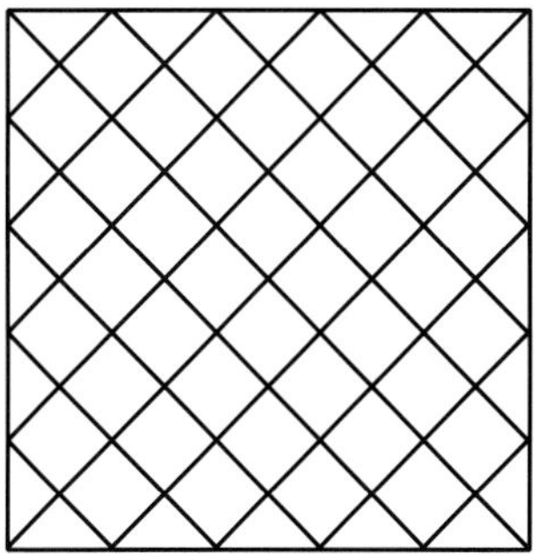

Kuiki lau, or echo quilting, has become the typical way to finish a Hawaiian quilt. However, there are many other quilting patterns that have been used over the years. The *i'e kuku,* or *tapa* beater, is the source of several of these patterns, including Ha'ao, Iwi-puhi, Hālu'a 'upena, Maka 'upena, and 'Upena pupu.

Other quilting patterns seen in older Hawaiian quilts include Kuiki lala, Papa'a pelena, Maka moena and Kuiki kuahonu.

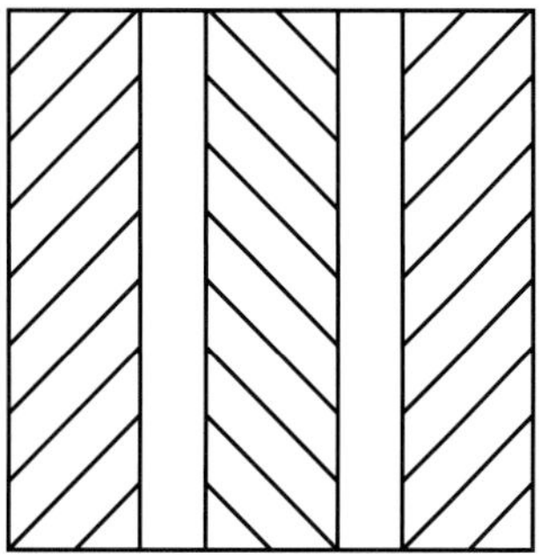

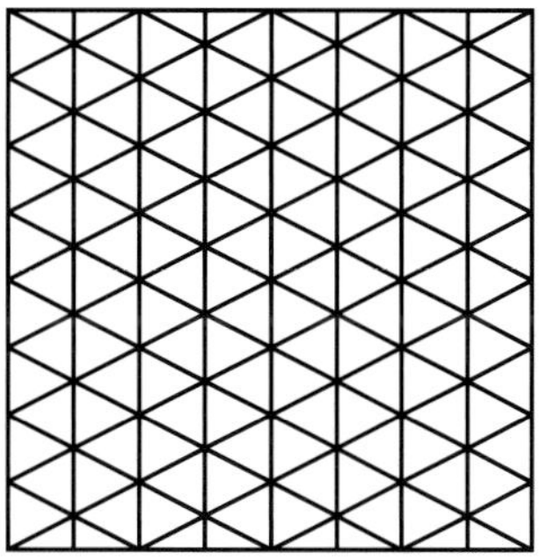

Maka 'upena (p. 86)

'Upena pupu (p. 87)

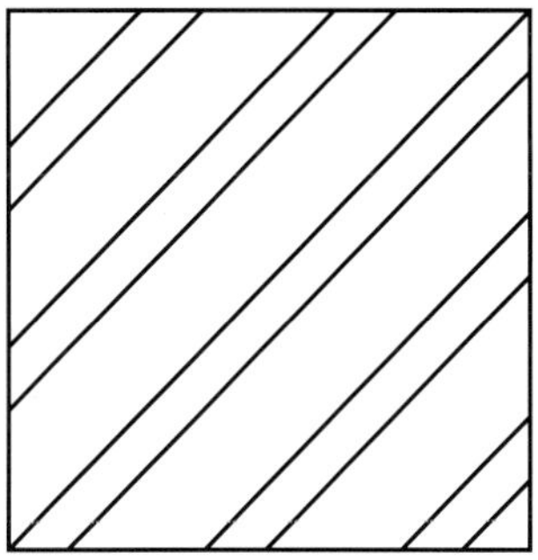

Kuiki lulu (p. 88)

Pāpa'a pelena (p. 89)

Maka moena (p. 90)

Kuiki kuahonu (p.91)

Hā'ao

zigzag

Iwi-puhi

eel bone

Iwi-puhi

eel bone, second version

Hālu'a 'upena

fish net

Enlarge pattern 200%

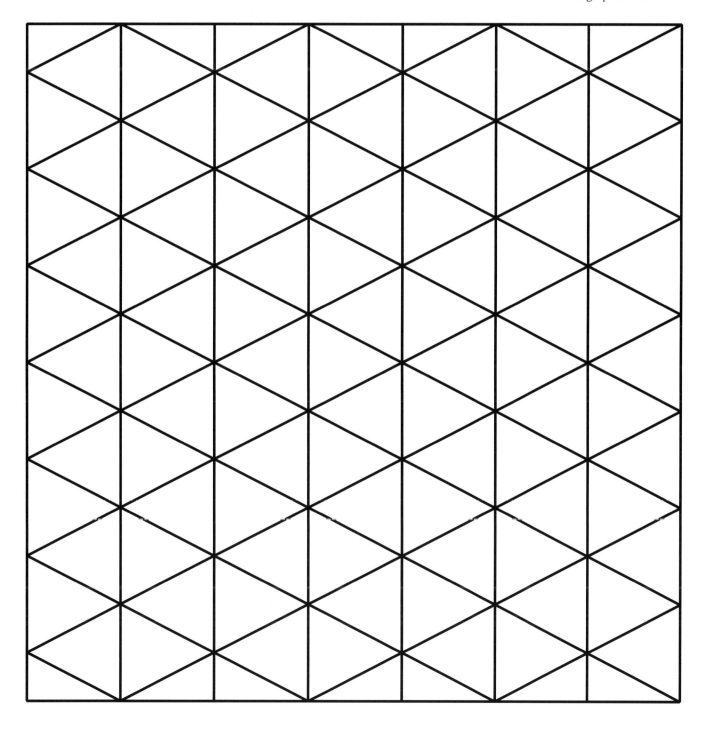

Maka 'upena

fish net mesh

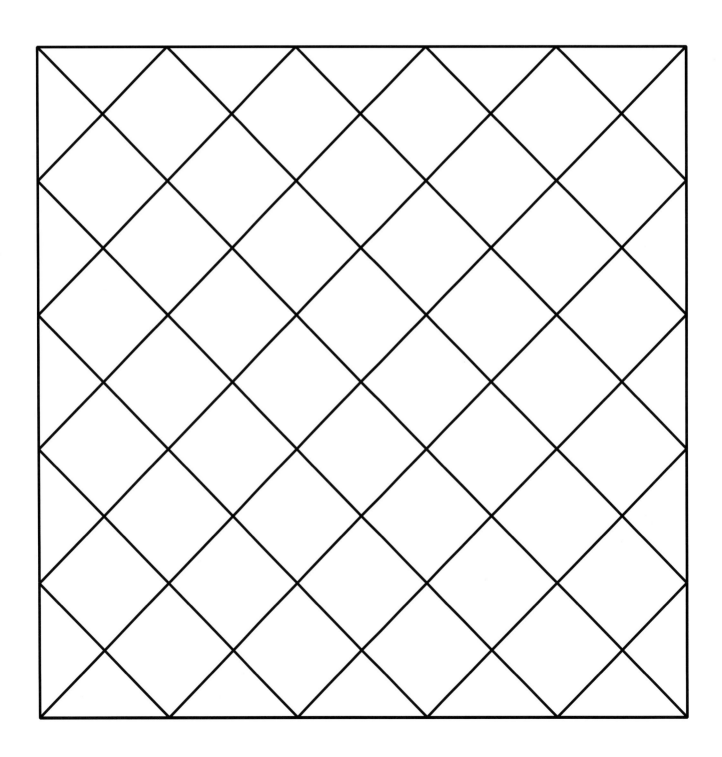

'Upena pupu

fish net with circles

Kuiki lala

diagonal lines

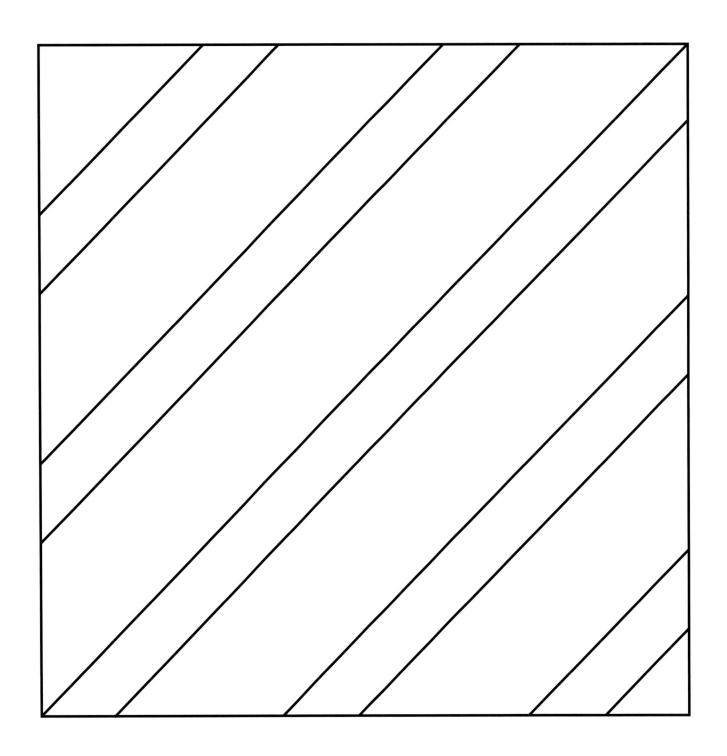

Pāpa'a pelena

soda cracker

Maka moena

lau hala mat mesh

Kuiki kuahonu

turtle's back

Enlarge pattern 200%

Bibliography

Books and Magazine Articles

Akana, Elizabeth. *Hawaiian Quilting: A Fine Art*. Honolulu: Hawaiian Mission Children's Society, 1981.

Akana, Elizabeth. "Ku'u Hae Aloha," *The Quilt Digest 2* (1984).

Arthur, Linda, PhD. *At the Cutting Edge: Contemporary Hawaiian Quilting*. Waipahu: Island Heritage Publishing, 2002.

Brandon, Reiko Mochinaga, and Honolulu Academy of Arts. *The Hawaiian Quilt*. Tokyo: Kokusai Art, 1989.

Dewhurst, C. Kurt, and Marsha L. MacDowell, eds. *To Honor and Comfort – Native Quilting Traditions*. Santa Fe: Museum of New Mexico Press, 1997.

Elbert, Samuel, and Mary Kawena Pukui. *Hawaiian Dictionary*. Honolulu: University of Hawai'i Press, 1986.

Fayé, Christine, and Margaret Lovett. *Kauai Museum Quilt Collection*. Lihue: Kauai Museum Publication, 1991.

Fleming, Vicky. "The Haole Connection," *Lady's Circle Patchwork Quilts,* March/April 1991.

Goforth, Sandra L. *Tutu and the Ti Plant*. Honolulu: MnM Publishing, 1993.

Goforth, Sandra L. *Tutu and the Ulu Tree*. Honolulu: MnM Publishing, 1994.

Guback, Georgia. *Luka's Quilt*. New York: Greenwillow Books, 1994.

Hammond, Joyce D. *Tifaifai and Quilts of Polynesia*. Honolulu: University of Hawai'i Press, 1986.

Jones, Stella M. *Hawaiian Quilts.* 1930. Reprint, revised. Honolulu: Daughters of Hawaii, Honolulu Academy of Arts and Mission Houses Museum, 1973.

Kakalia, Kepola. *Hawaiian Quilting as an Art.* Honolulu: Deborah U. Kakalia, 1976.

Kerr, Marge. "Hawaiian Periwinkle," *Quilter's Newsletter Magazine,* July/August, 1986.

Magee, Jan. "Island Beauties," *Quilter's Newsletter Magazine,* July/August, 2001.

Plews, Edith Rice. *Hawaiian Quilting on Kauai.* Lihue: Kaua'i Museum, 1976.

Rongokea, Lynnsay. *The Art of Tivaevae Traditional Cook Islands Quilting.* Honolulu: University of Hawai'i Press, 2001.

Root, Elizabeth. *Menehune Quilts. . . the Hawaiian Way.* Kailua: ERDHI (Elizabeth Root Designs Hawaii, Inc.), 2001.

Schleck, Robert J. *The Wilcox Quilts in Hawaii.* Lihui: Grove Farm Homestead and Waioli Mission House, 1986.

Serrao, Poakalani, and John Serrao. *The Hawaiian Quilt: A Spiritual Experience.* Honolulu: Mutual Publishing, 1997.

Shaw, Robert. *Hawaiian Quilt Masterpieces.* Westport, CT: Hugh Lauter Levin Associates, Inc., 1996.

Woodard, Loretta. "Hawaiian Outline-Embroidered Quilts," *Uncoverings* 18 (1997): 153-187. Research Papers of the American Quilt Study Group.

Video Cassettes

Oberosler, Sonja "Konia." *Welcome to My Garden: A Lesson in Traditional Hawaiian Quilting Techniques.* Captain Cook, 1993.

Tibbetts, Richard J. Jr., and Elaine Zinn. *The Hawaiian Quilt: A Cherished Tradition.* Honolulu, 1986.

Resources

It's more fun to go to Hawaii and collect all kinds of "things Hawaiian" in person, but since we can't all manage to do that, the Internet will have to be our vehicle for our Hawaiian shopping.

Just using your search engine, you'll find plenty of resources under "Hawaiian music," "Hawaiian fabric," and so on. I've found a couple of businesses that I particularly like.

For Hawaiian music, I shop www.mele.com. They have a huge selection of all kinds of Hawaiian music, plus some books and videos.

I started out over twenty years ago buying pillow patterns from Poakalani. She's still going strong, with a Web site full of quilt patterns in all sizes. Her address is www.nvo.com/poakalani. Another great source for patterns is www.quilthawaiian.com. They carry patterns from several designers.

For books about Hawaiian quilts, as well as great patterns, two Web sites top my list. From Hawaii is the site www.kwiltsnkoa.com. They have a few quilter's gift items also. Nancy Lee Chong's Web site is www.pacificrimquilts.com. She has loads of books and features her own quilt patterns, which you may have seen in some catalogs.

Just for fun, check out www.geocities.com/~olelo/. It's packed with information about the Hawaiian language (*olelo*).

About the Author

Vicky Fleming's orientation to the tropics began at an early age. When she was in third or fourth grade in Michigan, her teacher asked if east was to the left or right. Vicky answered, "Left." The teacher wouldn't budge on insisting that Vicky had given the wrong answer. The teacher hadn't specified "on the map," however, and in Vicky's mind, she was standing in Michigan looking toward Florida, so east was indeed on the left.

In her late twenties, Vicky found herself high and dry in landlocked Colorado. On her first trip to Hawaii, in 1980, she fell in love with the moist, fragrant islands. She had enjoyed needlework all her life, so, after she returned to Colorado, taking up Hawaiian quilting was a natural.

Hawaiian quilting gave Vicky a way to stay connected to the tropics. She joined the "Ha'ole Connection" quilt group to quilt Hawaiian and share stories and information on Hawaiian topics once a month. Marge Kerr, who started the group, taught most of the members how to do the craft. Auntie Debbie Kakalia was their "Hawaiian Connection."

In 1993, Vicky moved to Florida. Because there are so many parallels between life in Hawaii and Florida, Vicky feels she is more aware than ever of how the *kama'āina* (locals) of Hawaii live, and the encroachment of the modern way of life upon the natural world.

Vicky continues to enjoy Hawaiian quilting, as well as pursuing art quilt ideas. Vicky is a member of Peace River Quilt Guild. She and her husband own a 35-foot sailboat, which takes up whatever time isn't spent quilting.

Other AQS Books

This is only a small selection of the books available from the American Quilter's Society. AQS books are known worldwide for timely topics, clear writing, beautiful color photos, and accurate illustrations and patterns. The following books are available from your local bookseller, quilt shop, or public library.

#6415   us$29.95

#6077   us$24.95

#6211   us$19.95

#6300   us$24.95

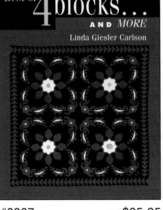

#6297   us$25.95

#5706   us$18.95

#6408   us$22.95

#6301   us$18.95

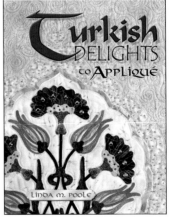

#6004   us$22.95

LOOK for these books nationally. CALL **1-800-626-5420**
or VISIT our Web site at **www.AQSquilt.com**